English Abused

Peter Beaven

with Christian Waters and William Sampson

English Abused

Peter Beaven, with Christian Waters and William Sampson

Editors: Deepak Joglekar and Donald St. John

Version 2.0 Revised: 21 April 2020

Published by

The Cheshire Press

an imprint of The Cheshire Group

Andover, MA 01810

www.cheshirepress.com

All rights reserved. No part of this book may be reproduced or transmitted in any form or by any means without the express written consent of the author, except for the inclusion of quotations in reviews.

Copyright ©2020 by Beaven & Associates

ISBN: 978-1-7327489-2-7

Library of Congress Control Number: 2020907667

Printed in the United States of America

Beaven & Associates

3 Dundee Park, #202 A

Andover, MA 01810

978 475-5487

www.beavenandassociates.com

Beaven, Peter

English Abused

The Applicant Seeks Employment

The Employer   *Regarding the cover letter you sent me for an opening in our company, I will read back what you wrote:*

Startups, Inc.   2/22/22
Personal Department
Dear Sirs,

The skill set of your workers in conjecture with mine would have quite a positive affect. They will be complimentary. They will raise to any challenge. My professors were after all imminent in their field and quite imaginary. Thank you, Brandon.

By personal do you mean personnel?

When you say, "in conjecture to mine," are you making a guess?

By "affect," do you mean "effect"?
By "complimentary," do you mean you will work for free? Perhaps you mean "complementary" with an "e" in the middle.

When you say, "raise to any challenge," do you mean someone will raise your salary? Perhaps you mean that you, yourself, will "rise" to any challenge?

Do you mean that your professors are "eminent' instead of "imminent"? If the latter, are your professors just about to arrive here to pay us a visit?

Were your professors "imaginative" like Steve Jobs, or perhaps "imaginary," like Harry Potter?

The Applicant   OMG. Do you mean malware and props are my bad? Not me. Never use em. Are you inferring to me that I do? By "diction," maybe you mean "dictionary"? In all due respective, all I want's a good paying job comeasurement with my skills which guys tell me are very affective.

The Employer   *Would you agree that an applicant should evince strong writing skills? In English Abused, the chapter called Diction, shows one how to avoid malapropisms and other pitfalls in word choice.*

English Abused

DEDICATED TO THE APPLICANT

After years in a classroom, the senior at last metamorphoses from student into applicant. Whether he ventures into the office of admissions, or the world of work—punctual and well-groomed—he will knock on a door for an interview. He will shake the hand of his greeter, whose clear, sharp diction prompts him to be businesslike and formal. His host will ask him how he might benefit the enterprise. The applicant must articulate his most positive response.

Even before the interview, however, the applicant must take pains to merit one. He must state in writing who he is, where he is going, and what he may offer. Thus, whether in admissions or personnel, an officer will read what the applicant writes and decide whether to grant an interview, or a banker will opt whether to grant a startup loan. Armed with effective writing skills, an applicant may persuade the school, business, or bank to open the door to opportunity. At a crossroads in his career—if not well before then—the applicant can learn just what to avoid from English Abused, and conversely what to acquire from the series *Crafting Sharper, Stronger English*.

English Abused

A student striving to be an effective writer needs practice putting his thoughts on paper. Whether in letters, journal entries, reports, compositions, or essays — he will hone his skills over time, learning by doing. To undergird his progress, however, he should know the fundamentals of English: its structure, grammar, syntax, usage, and idiosyncrasies. To avoid pitfalls that can drag him down and to make his work sharper and stronger, the aspiring writer might well avail himself of English Abused.

A Note About
The Series Crafting Sharper, Stronger English

At the base of all languages lie fundamental principles. Speakers and writers of a language neglect these principles at the risk of muddled communication. In most countries, instruction in these principles is mandatory. The government insists and the culture encourages. Today in the United States, however, schools far too often sidestep instruction in English fundamentals. As a result, a graduate of our systems enters the job market oblivious to the rigors of English, subject to its pitfalls, and yet required to articulate in cover letters and resumes, who he is as an individual and what he will contribute to a particular company. The graduate describes. However, the employer decides. The student with mediocre English is at pains to be convincing. Even a clever high tech graduate launching a start up will find out that his bright ideas expressed in fuzzy proposals do not carry the day with investors. Smart ideas badly articulated do not win loans.

In American schools a generation ago, students learned how each part of a sentence functioned, where each part belonged, and how a strong sentence with clear thinking must rescue a weak one. Students learned that a sentence contains a subject, a verb, prepositions, phrases, clauses, and other parts. In the opening line of the quaint song below, students could, for example, identify each part and know its function within the whole.

Over the river and through the woods
to grandmother's house we go.

Students today, however, regard such a skill to be as quaint and antiquarian as the song itself. Asked to identify the subject, modern students conflate it with a trip to grandmother's, prepositions with propositions, phrases with phases, clauses with tigers' paws, and sentences with a judge's orders. Students lack the verbal background that years ago their peers acquired in school and could rely on at the start of and throughout their careers.

English grammar, syntax, and composition are not easy to master, even for native speakers. Imagine, then, the challenges that confront today's Language Arts teachers in classrooms filled with a mix of native and non-native speakers. During four decades of tutoring middle and high school students seeking admission to top secondary schools and colleges, the tutors at Beaven & Associates have found that even private school pupils in small homogeneous classes may struggle with the finer points of usage and composition.

Popular Culture and the computer revolution are not helping. Children today spend far less time reading books than watching television, playing electronic games, and texting. Contemporary books, which must compete with electronic media for children's attention, are more likely to be filled with conversational slang than with the complex sentences and rich vocabulary of earlier children's classics. The same advances that have led to an information explosion have resulted in an implosion of grammatical knowledge.

Hence the development of the Crafting Sharper, Stronger English series; *English Structure, The English Sentence Up Close, English Abused,* and *English Mastery*. The series teaches the rules of grammar, syntax, and writing in a clear and systematic way. These books also serve as workbooks, with plentiful exercises to help students identify and remedy their weak points. In the short term, the books will help middle school, high school, and even college students perform better on standardized admissions tests, such as the HSPT, SSAT, PSAT, SAT, GMAT, GRE, and LSAT. More importantly, the books prepare a strong foundation for the communication skills that will serve students throughout their lives. An attempt to redress the loss of instruction in the fundamental of English is the series Crafting Sharper, Stronger English.

Table of Contents

Structure **6**
    The Parts of Speech Diagrammed 7
    The Parts of Speech in Text 23
    Phrases and Clauses 59

Grammar **69**
    Problems with Verbs 70
    Subject-Verb Agreement 82
    Pronouns 96
    Fragments 112

First Cumulative Review **119**

Syntax **132**
    Misplaced Modifiers and Dangling Element 133
    Parallel Structure 141

Second Cumulative Review **158**

Usage **171**
    Punctuation 172
    Restrictive and Nonrestrictive Elements 184
    Run-on Sentences 191
    Diction 200
    Wordiness 218

Third Cumulative Review **225**

Transitions in Writing Paragraphs **240**

STRUCTURE

Structure

Building Blocks of the Simple Sentence
The Parts of Speech Diagrammed

Diagramming

The students were studying.

```
 students  |  were studying
    \The
```

We follow rules.

```
  We  |  follow  |  rules
```

Haste makes waste.

```
  Haste  |  makes  |  waste
```

Throughout English Abused, the diagramming of sentences will be introduced the better to show a student English structure, grammar, syntax, and usage. Diagramming will be a visual tool to throw into relief, as though projecting onto a screen, not only the fundamentals of the language, but also its many pitfalls to be avoided. Seeing a diagram on paper, and then in the mind's eye, will help a student pursue excellence and mastery in Crafting Sharper, Stronger English.

View the examples and then complete the practice. Answers are at the end of the unit.

Intransitive verbs

A *transitive* verb is an action verb that can *act directly* on an object; an *intransitive can act* on an object *only indirectly*.

Example:	Practice:
Dogs growl. 　Dogs ｜ growl 　――――｜―――― *Dogs* is the subject of the sentence. Growl is a verb that shows action.	Cats purr. 　――――｜―――― 　　　　｜
She can run. 　――――｜―――― 　　　　｜ *Can* is a helping verb that indicates *she,* the subject, has the capability to run.	We could sleep. 　――――｜―――― 　　　　｜
They do eat. 　They ｜ do 　――――｜―――― 　　　　｜ sleep The helping verb *do* adds emphasis to the action verb.	Kangaroos do jump. 　――――｜―――― 　　　　｜
You must laugh. 　――――｜―――― 　　　　｜ The pronoun *you* functions as the subject of the sentence. The verb is *must laugh.* The helping verb *must* shows obligation.	She must know. 　――――｜―――― 　　　　｜

Shall we remain? we | Shall remain The pronoun *we* is the subject, and the verb is *shall remain*. *Shall* is capitalized because it is the first word in the sentence.	Should we creep? ———|———

Transitive Verbs

A transitive verb expresses an action directed toward a person or thing, thus it takes a direct object.

Example:	Practice:
We follow rules. We | follow | rules The pronoun *We* is the subject. *Follows* is the transitive verb; its direct object is *rules*.	Maurice likes soccer. ———|———|———
Bob is hitting Joe. ———|———|——— Bob, a proper noun, is the subject of the sentence. *Is hitting* is the transitive verb, and *Joe* is the direct object.	David is repairing cars. ———|———|———
Haste makes waste. Haste | makes | waste *Haste*, which is a noun, is the subject of the sentence. The transitive verb is *makes*, and *waste* is the direct object.	Airbags save lives. ———|———|———
Curtains block light. Curtains | block | light *Curtains* is the subject of the sentence. *Block* is the transitive verb; its direct object is *light*.	Scissors can cut paper. ———|———|———

Do you like pasta?

| you | Do like | pasta |

The pronoun *you* is the subject. The words *do like* act as the transitive verb, with *do* being a helping verb used for emphasis. *Pasta* is the direct object.

Will you bake cakes?

Articles

An adjective is a word that modifies a person place or thing. Articles are a type of adjective that define a subject as specific or unspecific. The definite article, *the*, is specific; the indefinite articles, *a, an, or some* are unspecific.

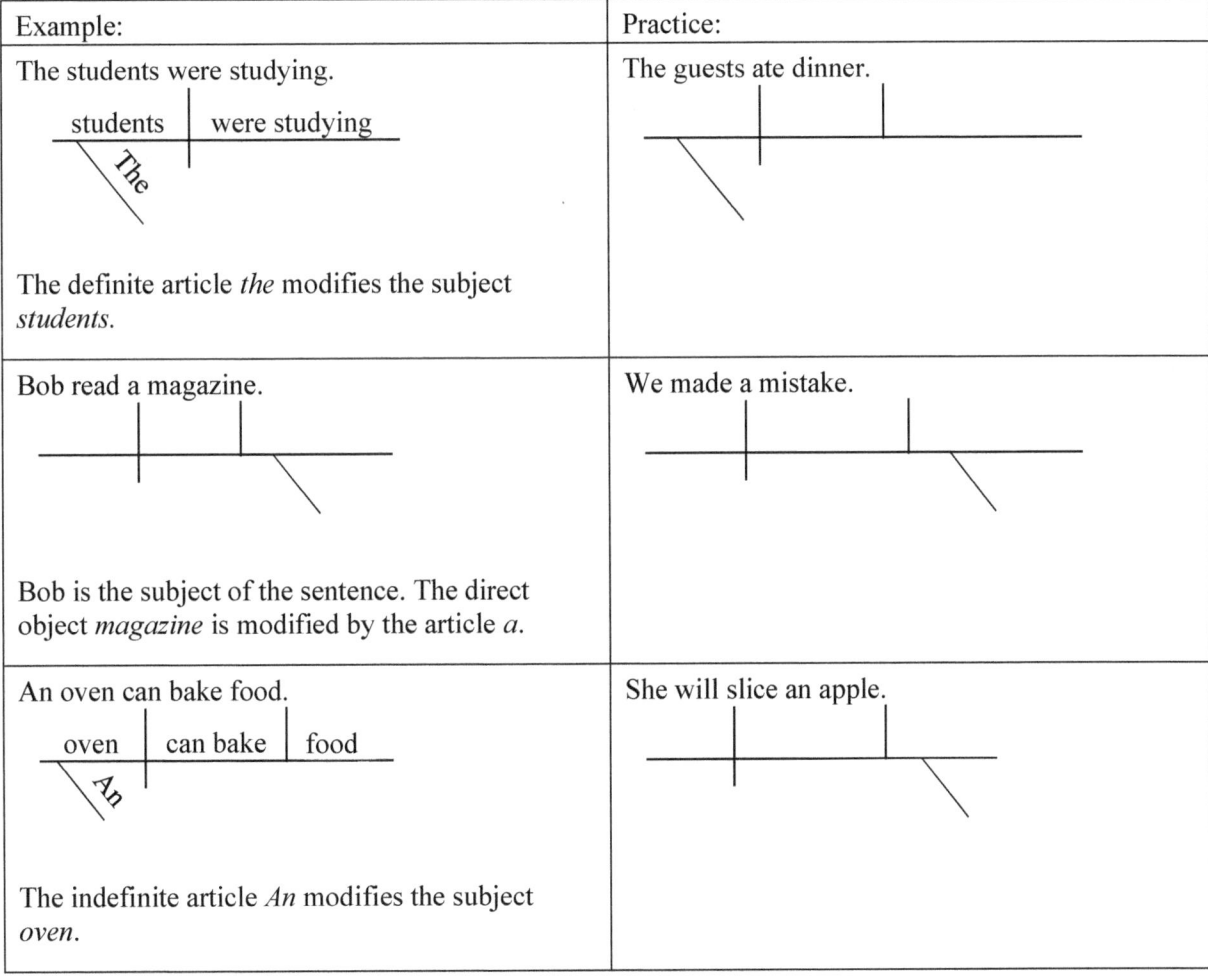

Example:

The students were studying.

| students | were studying |
\The

The definite article *the* modifies the subject *students*.

Practice:

The guests ate dinner.

Bob read a magazine.

Bob is the subject of the sentence. The direct object *magazine* is modified by the article *a*.

We made a mistake.

An oven can bake food.

| oven | can bake | food |
\An

The indefinite article *An* modifies the subject *oven*.

She will slice an apple.

Some girls are laughing. 　　girls │ are laughing 　　＼Some *Some* is an indefinite article which modifies *girls*.	We ate some chips.
Did you bring an umbrella? 　you │ Did bring │ umbrella 　　　　　　　　　　＼an The direct object *umbrella* is modified by the indefinite article *an*.	Will the computer work?

Adjectives

Adjectives modify or describe nouns. If there is more than one adjective describing a noun, they are placed in the order of occurrence.

Example:	Practice:
The haunted house was creaking. 　　house │ was creaking 　＼The ＼haunted The adjective *haunted* modifies the subject of the sentence *house*.	The bright full moon will show.
He read an interesting book. 　He │ read │ book 　　　　　　　＼an ＼interesting The adjective *interesting* modifies the direct object *book*.	She climbed the steep staircase

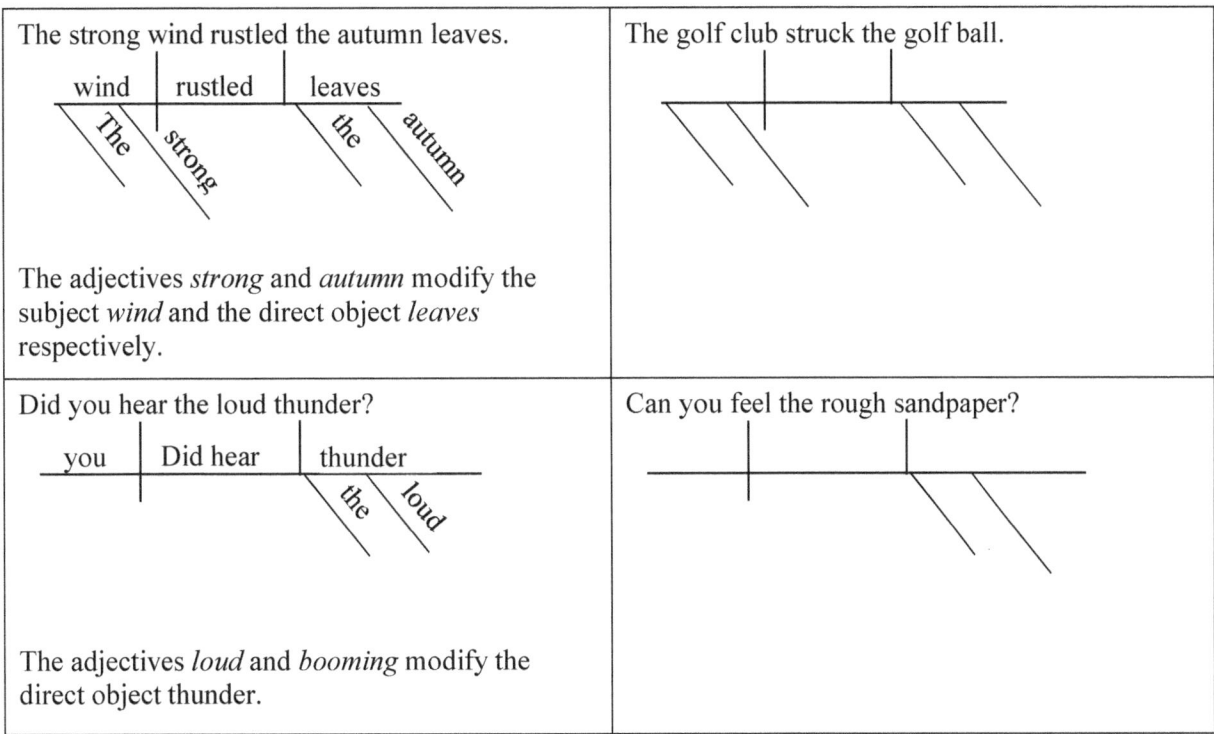

Adverbs I

Adverbs can modify a verb, an adjective, or another adverb. Adverbs answer these questions: How? To what extent? Where? When? This section contains adverbs that answer How? and To what extent?

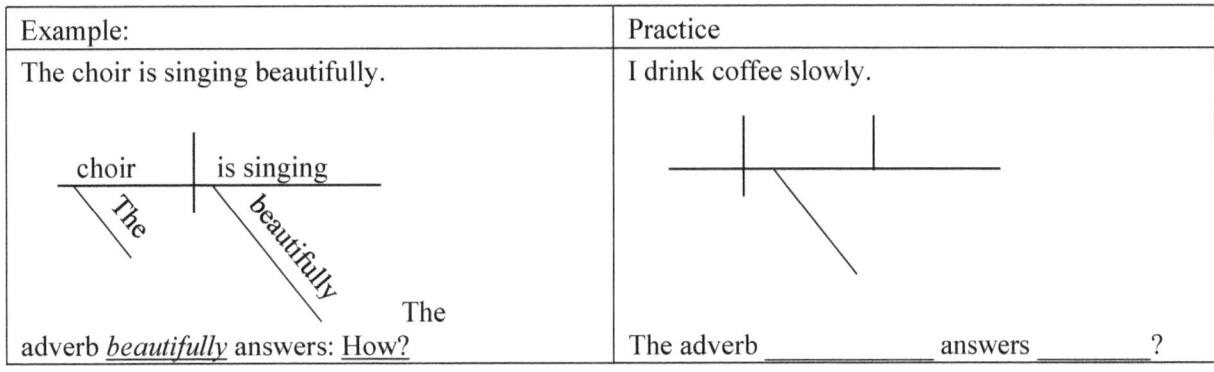

Very athletic people train frequently. people | train 　\\athletic　\\frequently 　　\\Very The adverb *very* answers: To what extent? *frequently* answers: To what extent?	We read an incredibly interesting novel. 　|　| 　　\\　\\ 　　　\\ The adverb _____ answers _____?
We swam very quickly. We | swam 　　\\quickly 　　\\very The adverb *very* answers: To what extent? The adverb *quickly* answers: How?	The thunder boomed very loudly. 　| 　　\\ 　　\\ The adverb _____ answers _____? The adverb _____ answers _____?
Do you fully understand the consequences? you | Do understand | consequences 　　　\\fully　　　　\\the The adverb *fully* answers: To what extent?	Does she not understand? 　| 　\\ The adverb _____ answers _____?

Adverbs II

This section contains adverbs that answer Where? and When? Sometimes, a noun can act as an adverb and answer the same questions adverbs answer.

Example:	Practice
I will finish my project tomorrow. *Tomorrow* is a noun used as an adverb that modifies the verb *finish*. The adverb *tomorrow* answers: When?	Summer is arriving soon. The adverb _____ answers _____?
Sally never practices piano. The adverb *never* answers: When?	She still teaches English. The adverb _____ answers _____?
We can go anywhere. The verb *go* is modified by *anywhere*, which is a noun used as an adverb. The adverb *anywhere* answers: Where?	My friend lives nearby. The adverb _____ answers _____?
Can we walk home now? The adverb *home* answers: Where? The adverb *now* answers: When?	Are you eating here? The adverb _____ answers _____?

Being (Linking) Verbs

Being verbs do not express action by a subject. Essentially, being verbs act as equal signs between a subject and a paired descriptive term.

Common being verbs:

Being Verbs:	is	am	are	were	be
Other being verbs:	appear	seem	taste	become	look
	feel	remain	sound	being	smell

When any *being* verb, stands alone, it is always a linking verb. Other verbs, can either act as a being verb or an action verb. If the verb can be replaced with an equal sign and the sentence still makes sense, then the verb is a being verb.

Example:	Practice:
John smells bad. _____John = bad_____ Replace the verb, *smells,* with an equal sign. Does the sentence makes sense? Yes. *smells* is a <u>being</u> verb	Your house seems big. _____ _____ is (a/an) _____ verb
John smells pizza. ~~_____John = pizza_____~~ Replace the verb, *smells,* with an equal sign. Does the sentence makes sense? No. *John* is not equal to *pizza*. *Smells* is an <u>action</u> verb	Jacob tasted sugar, _____ _____ is (a/an) _____ verb
Rhonda tastes the milk. ~~_____Rhonda = milk_____~~ Replace the verb, *tastes,* with an equal sign. Does the sentence makes sense? No. *Rhonda* is not equal to *milk*. *tastes* is an <u>action</u> verb	She smelled a gas leak. _____ _____ is (a/an) _____ verb
Milk tastes sour. _____Milk = sour_____ Replace the verb, *tastes,* with an equal sign. Does the sentence makes sense? Yes. *tastes* is a <u>being</u> verb	You look tired. _____ _____ is (a/an) _____ verb

Object Pronouns

A pronoun is a word that can take the place of a noun. Subject pronouns and object pronouns are "*personal pronouns*". An object pronoun replaces a direct or indirect object.

	Subject Pronouns		**Object Pronouns**	
Person	Singular	Plural	Singular	Plural
1st	I	we	me	us
2nd	you	you	you	you
3rd	he, she, it	they	him, her, it	them

Example:	Practice:
I love you. *You* is the objective pronoun acting as the direct object.	Ben must have stolen it.
Harry did not invite them. Harry | did invite | them \ not The objective pronoun is *them. Not* is an adverb modifying the verb *did invite*.	I have seen him before.
Can we meet her now? we | Can meet | her \ now *Her* is the direct object of the sentence; *her* is an objective pronoun.	Do you know me?
Can I help you? The objective pronoun *you* is the direct object.	Could you go help her?

Possessive Pronouns

A possessive pronoun denotes ownership.

	Singular	Plural
1st	mine	ours
2nd	yours	yours
3rd	his, hers, its	theirs

Example:	Practice:
These books are mine. Mine is the possessive pronoun in the sentence.	This gift is yours.
That computer is hers. computer | is \ hers \That In this sentence, the possessive pronoun is *hers*.	These shoes will be his.
That school is ours. school | is \ ours \That *Ours* is the possessive pronoun in the sentence.	That house is theirs.
Are those gloves mine? gloves | Are \ mine \those *Mine* is the possessive pronoun.	Is that red sweatshirt yours?

Diagramming Answers

Intransitive Verbs Answers

Cats purr.

Cats	purr

We could sleep.

We	could sleep

Kangaroos do jump.

Kangaroos	do jump

She must know.

She	must know

Should we creep?

we	Should creep

Transitive Verbs Answers

Maurice likes soccer.

Maurice	likes	soccer

David is repairing cars.

David	is repairing	cars

Airbags save lives.

Airbags	save	lives

Scissors can cut paper.

Scissors	can cut	paper

Will you bake cakes?

you	Will bake	cakes

Articles Answers

The guests ate dinner.

We made a mistake.

She will slice an apple.

We ate some chips.

Will the computer work?

Adjectives Answers

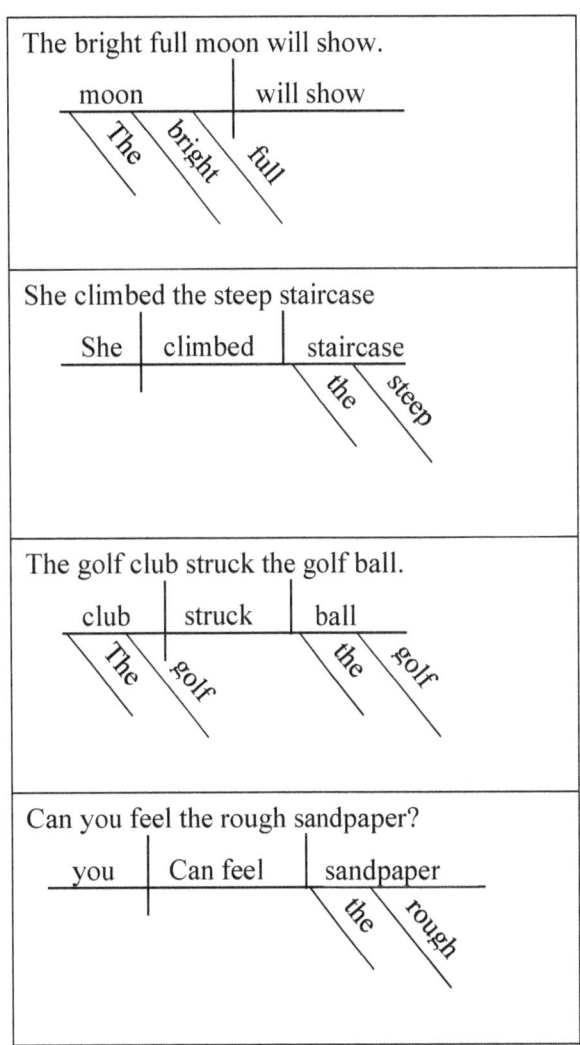

20

Adverbs I Answers

I drink coffee slowly.

I | drink | coffee
                \ slowly

The adverb *slowly* answers How?

We read an incredibly interesting novel.

We | read | novel
              \ an \ interesting
                         \ incredibly

The adjective *interesting* describes *novel*.
The adverb *incredibly* answers To what extent?

The thunder boomed very loudly.

thunder | boomed
   \ The   \ loudly
                 \ very

The adverb *loudly* answers How?
The adverb *very* answers To what extent?

Does she not understand?

she | Does understand
            \ not

The adverb *not* answers To what extent?

Adverbs II Answers

Summer is arriving soon.

Summer | is arriving
               \ soon

The adverb *soon* answers When?

She still teaches English.

She | teaches | English
          \ still

The adverb *still* answers When?

My friend lives nearby.

friend | lives
  \ My   \ nearby

The adverb *nearby* answers Where?

Are you eating here?

you | Are eating
           \ here

The adverb *here* answers Where?

Being Verbs Answers

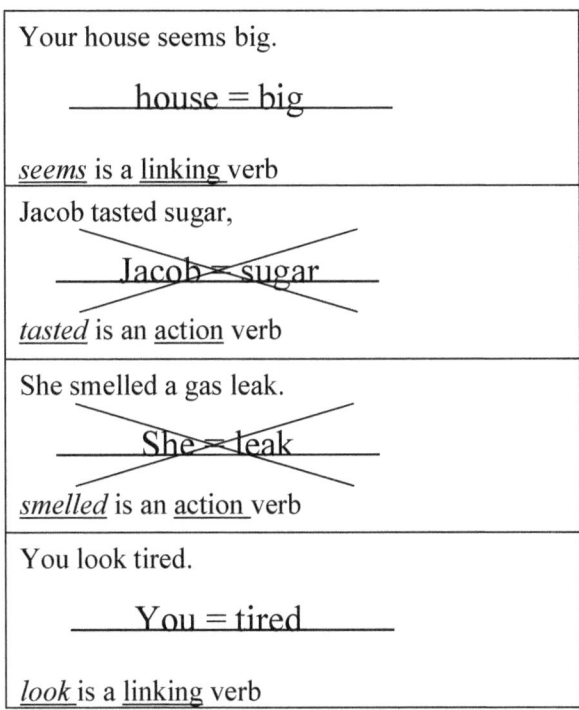

Objective Pronouns Answers

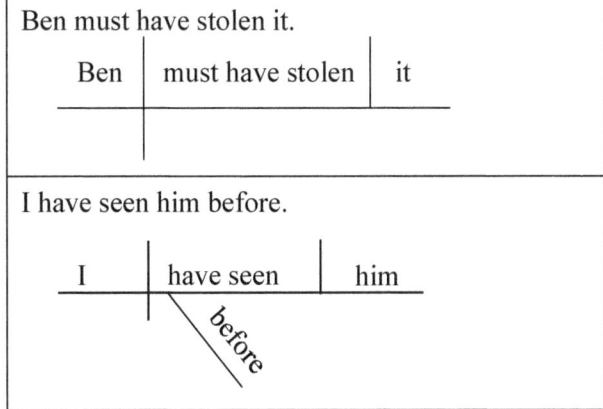

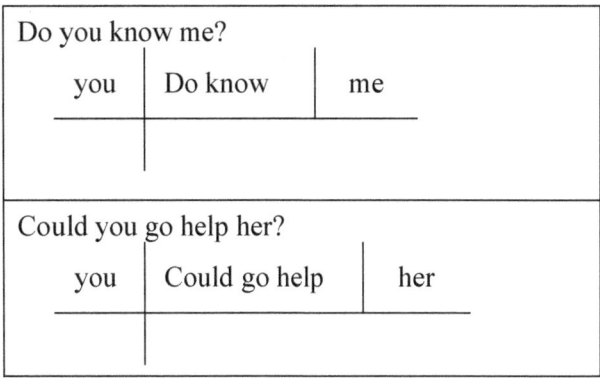

Possessive Pronouns

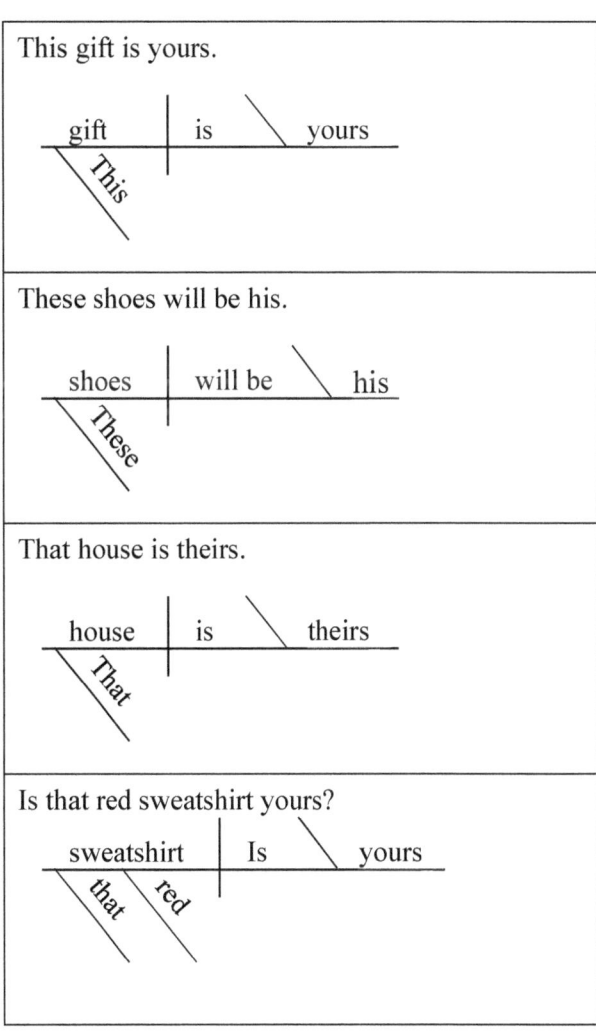

Structure Continued

The Building Blocks of the Simple Sentence

The Parts of Speech in Text

I. The Sentence

A sentence is a group of words that expresses a complete thought.

II. Nouns

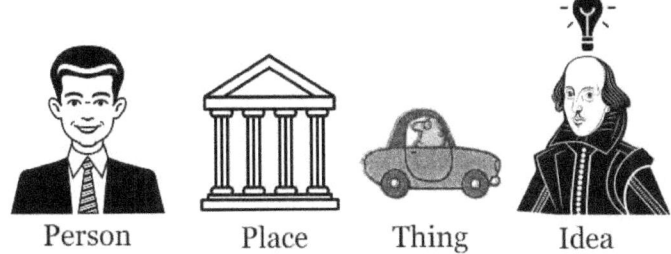

Person   Place   Thing   Idea

A. The Role of a Noun in a Sentence

Nouns answer the questions who or what. The noun in a sentence is the person, place, thing, or idea that initiates the thought of the sentence.

If we say, "Dogs bark," then "Dogs" is the noun that initiates the thought and, as such, is called the ***subject*** of the sentence.

Dogs bark.   *Dogs* is the subject.

Nouns can also **receive** the action. If we say, "Dogs chase wheels", the "wheels" receive the action of "Dogs." When a noun receives the action, that noun is considered the ***object***.

Dogs chase **wheels**.   *wheels* is the object.

An ***indirect object*** is the recipient of the subject and answers: *to what? for what? to whom?* or *for whom?* If Sarah made John cookies, *John* is the ***indirect object*** because he is receiving *cookies*.

Sarah made **John** cookies.   *John* is the indirect object.

Drill 1 *Identify each subject (S), direct object (D) and indirect object (I) in the following sentences.*

1. Employees earn salaries.
2. French monarchs gave Avignon Popes orders.
3. Music plays.
4. We sent my brother a present.
5. Joe punched the bartender.
6. Squirrels climb trees.
7. The factory makes the retailer hats.
8. We drove.
9. I always visit my sister at college.
10. Michael earned an internship.

B. Types of Nouns

Nouns can be classified into the following subcategories:

Concrete / Abstract	<ul><li>**Concrete**: anything that is tangible or discernable by sense<ul><li>*door, computer, light, sound, electricity*</li></ul></li><li>**Abstract**: anything that is intangible: ideas, beliefs, qualities, etc.<ul><li>*love, hatred, exasperation, fatigue, capitalism, Judaism*</li></ul></li></ul>
Proper / Common	<ul><li>**Proper**: refers to a specific person, place, or thing; capitalized<ul><li>*Niagara Falls, George Lucas, Coca-Cola, Forrest Gump*</li></ul></li><li>**Common**: refers to any non-specific person, place, or thing<ul><li>*goat, audacity, father, treehouse, violence*</li></ul></li></ul>
Singular / Plural	<ul><li>**Singular**: refers to only one noun or entity<ul><li>*monitor, piece, clock, ox*</li></ul></li><li>**Plural**: references two or more of the same noun<ul><li>*monitors, pieces, clocks, oxen*</li></ul></li></ul>
Collective	<ul><li>**Collective**: names a group; usually treated as a single entity<ul><li>*band, team, association, committee, herd*</li></ul></li><li>**Not Collective**: names an individual person, place, or thing<ul><li>*man, chair, building, Zionism, movement*</li></ul></li></ul>

Drill 2

Identify and underline each of the 37 nouns in this passage excerpted from Charles Dickens's The Pickwick Papers.

"We write these words now, many miles distant from the spot at which, year after year, we met on that day, a merry and joyous circle. Many of the hearts that throbbed so gaily then, have ceased to beat; many of the looks that shone so brightly then, have ceased to glow; the hands we grasped, have grown cold; the eyes we sought, have hid their lustre in the grave; and yet the old house, the room, the merry voices and smiling faces, the jest, the laugh, the most minute and trivial circumstances connected with those happy meetings, crowd upon our mind at each recurrence of the season, as if the last assemblage had been but yesterday! Happy, happy Christmas, that can win us back to the delusions of our childish days; that can recall to the old man the pleasures of his youth; that can transport the sailor and the traveler, thousands of miles away, back to his own fireside and his quiet home!"

ANSWER KEY

Drill 1

1. Employees (S) earn salaries (D).
2. French monarchs (S) gave Avignon Popes (I) orders (D).
3. Music (S) plays.
4. We (S) sent my brother (I) a present (D).
5. Joe (S) punched the bartender (D).
6. Squirrels (S) climb trees (D).
7. The factory (S) makes the retailer (I) hats (D).
8. We (S) drove.
9. I (S) always visit my sister (D) at college.
10. Michael (S) earned an internship (D).

Drill 2

"We write these <u>words</u> now, many <u>miles</u> distant from the <u>spot</u> at which, <u>year</u> after <u>year</u>, we met on that <u>day</u>, a merry and joyous <u>circle</u>. Many of the <u>hearts</u> that throbbed so gaily then, have ceased to beat; many of the <u>looks</u> that shone so brightly then, have ceased to glow; the <u>hands</u> we grasped, have grown cold; the <u>eyes</u> we sought, have hid their <u>lustre</u> in the <u>grave</u>; and yet the old <u>house</u>, the <u>room</u>, the merry <u>voices</u> and smiling <u>faces</u>, the <u>jest</u>, the <u>laugh</u>, the most minute and trivial <u>circumstances</u> connected with those happy <u>meetings</u>, crowd upon our <u>mind</u> at each <u>recurrence</u> of the <u>season</u>, as if the last <u>assemblage</u> had been but yesterday! Happy, happy <u>Christmas</u>, that can win us back to the <u>delusions</u> of our childish <u>days</u>; that can recall to the old <u>man</u> the <u>pleasures</u> of his <u>youth</u>; that can transport the <u>sailor</u> and the <u>traveler</u>, <u>thousands</u> of <u>miles</u> away, back to his own <u>fireside</u> and his quiet <u>home</u>!"

III. Verbs

"To be, or not to be, that is the question:
Whether tis nobler in the mind to suffer
The slings and arrows of outrageous fortune,
Or take arms against a sea of troubles and by opposing
end them." -Shakespeare's Hamlet

Hamlet must decide whether to act or to be.

A sentence consists of a subject, a noun or pronoun—a person, place, or thing—and its verb, showing an action—"run," "grab," "enact"—or a state of being—"is," "appears," or "seems."

Classifications of Verbs

A. Action Verbs

Action verbs describe what a certain noun/subject **does**.

Some common action verbs are:

walk	run	eat	believe
think	help	strut	say
catch	throw	smell	call

Examples: Samantha *eats* cake.

The boy **said**, "Hello!"

The balloon **will pop**.

Intransitive Verbs
Intransitive verbs show actions, but the actions are not directed at an object. When soldiers fight, but are not fighting something, then "fight" is an intransitive verb.

Soldiers fight.

Transitive Verbs

A ***transitive verb*** expresses an action directed toward a person or thing; therefore, it takes a ***direct object***, the recipient of the action of a transitive verb. When soldiers fight enemies, they are fighting something, an object.

Soldiers fight **enemies**.

Drill 1 *Identify whether the sentence contains a transitive or intransitive verb.*

1. Criminals run.
2. Dogs chase cats.
3. Investors hope to profit from the upswing of stock values.
4. Prison sentences can be extended.
5. Whales swim.
6. Government policies affect commerce.
7. History determines culture.
8. Airplanes fly.
9. My old CD player doesn't work.
10. Jeff travels to Albuquerque.

B.   Linking Verbs

State of being verbs, or ***linking verbs***, do not express an action taken by the subject. Instead, they serve to <u>link the subject</u> with a descriptive term.

Whenever a linking verb is used to connect a subject and object, a ***predicate nominative*** or ***predicate adjective*** is created. The linking verb serves to rename the subject.

> A ***predicate nominative*** is a noun that follows a verb to specify or rename the subject. The logic behind the predicate nominative is that of logic found in algebra.
> If X = Y, then Y = X. If Joe is a bartender, the bartender is Joe. The verb shows no action. Rather, it expresses a simple state of being.

Examples:

Joe is a **bartender**.	***bartender*** is the predicate nominative.
Mr. Johnson remained **President**.	***President*** is the predicate nominative.
Mr. Johnson appeared **presidential**.	***presidential*** is the predicate adjective.

Some common linking verbs are:

appear	is	seem	taste
become	look	smell	grow
feel	remain	sound	stay

Some verbs can serve as an action verb and a linking verb. Consider the following examples.

Examples: The dog **smells** well.
(The dog has a good sense of smell.)

The dog **smells** good.
(*Smells* connects the subject, dog, to more information about its scent.)

Drill 2 *Identify the linking verbs and indicate whether a predicate nominative or predicate adjective follows.*

1. The girl is a student.
2. The water seemed cold.
3. The dog smells good.
4. That man will be a good professor.
5. She looks athletic.

C. Verb Tenses

Verb tenses describe when an action is happening, was happening, or will be happening.

Tense:	Examples:
Present	• I love running in the park. • He studies every school night. • The President delivers his State of the Union address at 7 p.m.
Past	• I gained admission to Harvard Law School yesterday. • She served in the Marines for five years.

Future	- I will submit the grievances this upcoming week. - If the tenant decides to withdraw prematurely from the leasing contract, she will lose five thousand dollars.
Present Progressive *Past Progressive* *Future Progressive*	- I am working. - I was working. - I will be working.
Present Perfect *Past Perfect* *Future Perfect*	- I have worked. - I had worked. - I will have worked.

Drill 3 *Identify the verb tenses of each of the following sentences.*

1. During the 16th century, several Jesuit priests in the Catholic Church advanced science with their own private research.

2. I will be the president of this company eventually.

3. She toured five colleges this week.

4. When I was driving to New Hampshire, my car suddenly caught on fire.

5. I have used various phone service providers, and I have determined that they are all inconsistent.

ANSWER KEYS

Drill 1

1. Intransitive
2. Transitive
3. Transitive
4. Intransitive
5. Intransitive
6. Transitive
7. Transitive
8. Intransitive
9. Intransitive
10. Intransitive

Drill 2

1. Linking Verb: is — Predicate nominative: student
2. Linking Verb: seemed — Predicate adjective: cold
3. Linking Verb: smells — Predicate adjective: good
4. Linking Verb: will be — Predicate nominative: professor
5. Linking Verb: looks — Predicate adjective: athletic

Drill 3

1. Past tense
2. Future tense
3. Past tense
4. Past progressive
5. Present perfect (both verbs)

IV. Pronouns

He　　　　　　She　　　　　　They

A pronoun is a word that takes the place of a noun.

A. Personal Pronouns

	Subject Pronouns		**Object Pronouns**	
Person	Singular	Plural	Singular	Plural
1st	I	we	me	us
2nd	you	you	you	you
3rd	he, she, it	they	him, her, it	them

Examples:

I love **you**.

(I is the subject pronoun, while you is the object pronoun, the direct object.)

Can **we** meet **her** now?

(The subject pronoun is we. Her is the direct object of the sentence; her is an object pronoun.)

She did not invite **them**.

(The subject pronoun is she. The object pronoun is them.)

Drill 1 *Identify all personal pronouns in the following sentences.*

1. I went to the mall.

2. Everyone is on the basketball team except for him.

3. Without her, I am sad.

4. They earned their bachelors and then they began their job searches.

5. We must send out a distress signal in order to be rescued from this island.

B. Possessive Pronouns

A possessive pronoun denotes ownership.

	Singular	**Plural**
1st	mine	ours
2nd	yours	yours
3rd	his, hers, its	theirs

Examples:

These books are mine.

(Mine is the possessive pronoun in the sentence.)

That school is ours.

(Ours is the possessive pronoun in the sentence.)

Drill 2 *Identify all possessive pronouns in the following sentences.*

1. The scholarship is his.

2. Is that phone yours?

3. Your problem is ours; we must fix the mismanagement of our office.

4. The house with the decaying walls is theirs.

5. Once we settle this class action lawsuit, we will have the money that is rightfully ours.

C. Indefinite Pronouns

Indefinite pronouns do not refer to any specific person, thing, or amount. But they must agree with their subjects in number and gender.

There are roughly 40 indefinite pronouns that fall into two categories:
- Those referring to a non-specific noun, such as *none, anybody, something, anything*.
- Those which are easily understood because they refer to a <u>previous</u> specific noun or are followed by explanatory words.

*My classmates are **all** girls. **Each** is wearing a dress or skirt.*

Such pronouns can also function as adjectives.

***All** girls carry purses. **Each** girl carried a purse.*

***Several** [pronoun] are fruits* vs. ***several** [adjective] fruits are.*

***Many** [pronoun] plan to go* vs. ***many** [adjective] friends plan to go.*

Some **singular indefinite pronouns** are: *another, anyone, each, everybody, one, everything*, and *no one*.

Every<u>one</u> should bring (**his/her**) own lunch.

Every<u>thing</u> has **its** price.

Some **plural indefinite pronouns** are: *both, few, many, most*, and *several*.

<u>Both</u> (choices) have **their** advantages.

<u>Most</u> (gentlemen) mind **their** manners.

It may not be obvious which *indefinite* pronouns are considered singular or plural. Some **indefinite pronouns may be singular or plural** depending on context, including: *all, any, none,* and *some.*

All noise has **its** value.   All noises cause **their** listeners problems.

Any mom can teach **her** kids.   Any moms can teach **their** kids.

Some virtue is **its** own reward.   Some virtues have **their** bad aspects.

None of the show was funny   None of the shows were funny

    in **its** opening act.   in **their** opening acts.

Drill 3 *Identify all indefinite pronouns in the following sentences.*

1. Freshman lawmakers in Washington, D.C., have much to learn.

2. Most of your friends will be invited to my party, but annoying ones will not.

3. My colleagues are very intelligent; several have worked as professors at Harvard University.

4. It seems like everything students learn in school is completely disconnected from the endeavors of life, such as filing taxes and balancing a checkbook.

5. Anything can be interpreted as hate speech.

D. Reflexive Pronouns

Reflexive pronouns reflect on their antecedents; that is, the pronoun refers to what it represents in the same clause. Consequently, the reflexive pronoun is itself never a subject.

The reflexive pronouns, all of which end in *-self* or *-selves*, include:

myself	ourselves	oneself
yourself	yourselves	himself
herself	itself	themselves

Reflexive pronouns rename or serve to intensify the subject. Such pronouns are properly used in any of three situations:

The subject and direct object are the same:

The priest crossed himself in front of the altar.

They shouldn't go out at night by themselves.

You should get yourself a wife.

I did it not for you but for myself.

One can hurt oneself playing with fire.

The subject and indirect object are the same:

"The mind is its own place, and in itself can make a heaven of hell, a hell of heaven."   -John Milton

Icy roads are not a problem in themselves.

The pronoun acts an **intensive pronoun** to emphasize the subject:

The queen herself made the announcement.

They all volunteered; I myself had no choice.

Drill 4 *Identify all reflexive pronouns in the following sentences.*

1. The campaign manager himself went door to door advocating for his candidate.

2. As a result of their juvenile actions, the four high schoolers found themselves in the vice principal's office.

3. When a government continues to take away the rights and liberties of citizens, the people themselves must act in defense of their freedoms.

4. The popular politician praises the redistribution of wealth, but he himself owns three multimillion-dollar homes.

5. He believed himself to be superior to his friends in every way.

E. Relative Pronouns

The relative pronouns who, whom, whoever, whomever, that, whose, which, and whichever:

The **relative pronouns who, whoever, whom** and **whomever** are used **only for people** as opposed to the pronoun **which. Which** is used when referring to other, non-person entities.

F. Interrogative Pronouns
The interrogative pronouns who, whom, whose, which, and what:

Interrogative pronouns are used for asking questions.

Who did he work for?

What was his mission?

Drill 5 *Identify and label the pronouns in the following series of sentences.*

Personal (PER), Possessive (POS), Indefinite (IND), Reflexive (REF), Relative (REL)

At various points during the 1980s and '90s, a mysterious source sent explosive packages to multiple technology firms. Eventually, FBI agents discovered that Ted Kaczynski, whose violent efforts had earned him the nickname "UnaBomber," had been hiding in a remote cabin in Montana from which he orchestrated his scheme. Investigators had wondered who helped Kaczynski and what he wanted. After numerous theories, it was discovered that Kaczynski, a mathematics genius who had attended both Harvard University and the University of Michigan, had decided to pit himself against technological progress of any kind. He operated alone, targeting anyone in charge of computer firms. All who worked in the realm of technology had been at risk during the UnaBomber's reign of terror. At one point, Kaczynski had even blackmailed the *New York Times* into releasing a lengthy essay. Some readers of the piece found themselves agreeing with its radical sentiments and labeled it *The UnaBomber Manifesto*. Most believed the writing to be insane. His is an unusual story, but Ted Kaczynski will live out the rest of his life behind bars.

ANSWER KEYS

Drill 1

1. I went to the mall.
2. Everyone is on the basketball team except for him.
3. Without her, I am sad.
4. They earned their bachelors and then began their job searches.
5. We must send out a distress signal in order to be rescued from this island.

Drill 2

1. The scholarship is his.
2. Is that phone yours?
3. Your problem is ours; we must fix the mismanagement of our office.
4. The house with the decaying walls is theirs.
5. Once we settle this class action lawsuit, we will have the money that is rightfully ours.

Drill 3

1. Freshman lawmakers in Washington, D.C. have much to learn.
2. Most of your friends will be invited to my party, but annoying ones will not.
3. My colleagues are very intelligent; several have worked as professors at Harvard University.
4. It seems like everything students learn in school is completely disconnected from the endeavors of life, such as filing taxes and balancing a checkbook.
5. Anything can be interpreted as hate speech.

Drill 4

1. The campaign manager himself went door to door advocating for his candidate.
2. As a result of their juvenile actions, the four high schoolers found themselves in the vice principal's office.
3. When a government continues to take away the rights and liberties of citizens, the people themselves must act in defense of their freedoms.
4. The popular politician praises the redistribution of wealth, but he himself owns three multimillion-dollar homes.
5. He believed himself to be superior to his friends in every way.

Drill 5

At various points during the 1980s and '90s, a mysterious source sent explosive packages to multiple technology firms. Eventually, FBI agents discovered that Ted Kaczynski, whose (REL) violent efforts had earned him the nickname "UnaBomber," had been hiding in a remote cabin in Montana from which (REL) he (PER) orchestrated his scheme. Investigators had wondered who (REL) helped Kaczynski and what (REL) he (PER) wanted. After numerous theories, it (PER) was discovered that Kaczynski, a mathematics genius who (REL) had attended both Harvard University and the University of Michigan, had decided to pit himself (REF) against technological progress of any kind. He (PER) operated alone, targeting anyone (IND) in charge of computer firms. All (IND) who (REL) worked in the realm of technology had been at risk during the UnaBomber's reign of terror. At one point, Kaczynski had even blackmailed the *New York Times* into releasing a lengthy essay. Some readers of the piece found themselves (REF) agreeing with its radical sentiments and labeled it *The UnaBomber Manifesto*. Most (IND) believed the writing to be insane. His (POS) is an unusual story, but Ted Kaczynski will live out the rest of his life behind bars.

V. Adjectives

Intelligent Musical Tall

Adjectives answer the following questions: what kind of? how many?

A. Articles

Articles are a type of adjective that define a subject as specific or unspecific. The definite article, *the*, is specific; the indefinite articles, *a, an, or some,* are unspecific.

Examples:

The students were studying.

(The definite article *The* modifies the subject *students*.)

Some girls are laughing.

(*Some* is an indefinite article that modifies *girls*.)

Drill 1 *Identify all articles in the following sentences.*

1. The criminals were running from the cops.

2. A disservice to the locals, the visitors' littering at the lake was increasing.

3. The ground was shaking as an elephant ran across the field.

4. Some students defer one year of college to pursue internships or to volunteer.

5. Do you see that man who is playing music near a gazebo?

B. Regular Adjectives

Adjectives modifying or describing nouns can be seen below.

Example:

> She wore sunscreen to protect herself from the hot sun.
>
> (The adjective *hot* modifies the noun *sun*.)
>
> The athletic man dunked the basketball.
>
> (The adjective *athletic* modifies the noun *man*.)

Drill 2 *Identify all regular adjectives in the following sentences.*

1. The ugly, green Martian descended from the sky in a transparent disc.
2. Enigmatic, de-facto rulers tend to draw the most public attention.
3. Wearing expensive suits and looking confident, the team of eccentric executives had their proposals harshly rejected by the stern company president.
4. Ally's favorite activity is driving her red convertible along the beautiful coastline.
5. The old computer, which had seen ten years of loyal service to its owner, finally malfunctioned in a final display of bright shocks and loud noises, indicating its end.

C. Demonstrative Adjectives

The four **demonstrative adjectives**—*this*, *that*, *these* and *those*—indicate proximity of a noun modified. *This* and *these* indicate a thing or things close at hand, while *that* and *those* refer to things more distant.

Examples:

> These shoes will fit.
>
> (*Shoes* is modified by the demonstrative *these*.)

That pencil has an eraser.

(The subject *pencil* is modified by the demonstrative adjective *that*.)

Drill 3 *Identify all demonstrative adjectives in the following sentences.*

1. Those directions will bring you to the wrong location; try these instead.
2. This phone has no service.
3. My favorite possession and the defining aspect of my life is that car: a 1999 Toyota Camry.
4. This company will not tolerate this type of reckless behavior, Mr. O'Sullivan.
5. Those buffoons just injured themselves while trying to use homemade fireworks.

D.   Predicate Adjectives

A *predicate adjective* is an adjective that follows the linking verb and describes the subject.

Examples:

Roses are red.

(*Are* is a linking verb because it is a being verb. *Red* is the predicate adjective because it describes the roses.)

Were they angry?

(The pronoun *they* is the subject of the sentence. *Angry* follows the verb *were* as the predicate adjective.)

E. Possessive Adjectives

Possessive adjectives show ownership or belonging of the modified noun. The possessive adjectives:

Person	Singular	Plural
1st	mine	ours
2nd	yours	yours
3rd	his, hers, its	theirs

Examples:

I love my dog.

(The possessive adjective *my* modifies the direct object *dog*.)

Our team can beat the opposition.

(The subject *team* is modified by the possessive adjective *our*.)

F. Participles

Participles are verbal adjectives. They demonstrate action while describing a subject.

Examples:

The increasing speed of the asteroid posed a threat to the Earth.

(The participle *increasing* modifies the noun *speed*.)

Larry's bruised collarbone prevented him from playing in the championship game.

(The participle *bruised* modifies the noun *collarbone*.)

Drill 4 *In the following passage from Emily Bronte's* Wuthering Heights, *underline all twelve adjectives and indicate what is modified. You do not have to underline articles or possessives.*

"The moon shone bright; a sprinkling of snow covered the ground, and I reflected that she might, possibly, have taken it into her head to walk about the garden, for refreshment. I did detect a figure creeping along the inner fence of the park; but it was not my young mistress: on its emerging into the light, I recognized one of the grooms. He stood a considerable period, viewing the carriage-road through the grounds; then started off at a brisk pace, as if he had detected something, and reappeared presently, leading Miss's pony; and there she was, just dismounted, and walking by its side. The man took his charge stealthily across the grass towards the stable. Cathy entered by the casement window of the drawing room, and glided noiselessly up to where I awaited her. She put the door gently to, slipped off her snowy shoes, untied her hat, and was proceeding, unconscious of my espionage, to lay aside her mantle, when I suddenly rose and revealed myself.

ANSWER KEY

Drill 1

1. <u>The</u> criminals were running from <u>the</u> cops.
2. <u>A</u> disservice to the locals, <u>the</u> visitors' littering at <u>the</u> lake was increasing.
3. <u>The</u> ground was shaking as <u>an</u> elephant ran across <u>the</u> field.
4. <u>Some</u> students defer one year of college to pursue internships or to volunteer.
5. Do you see that man who is playing music near <u>a</u> gazebo?

Drill 2

1. The <u>ugly</u>, <u>green</u> Martian descended from the sky in a <u>transparent</u> disc.
2. <u>Enigmatic</u>, <u>de-facto</u> rulers tend to draw the most <u>public</u> attention.
3. Wearing <u>expensive</u> suits and looking <u>confident</u>, the team of <u>eccentric</u> executives had their proposals harshly rejected by the <u>stern</u> company president.
4. Ally's <u>favorite</u> activity is driving her <u>red</u> convertible along the <u>beautiful</u> coastline.
5. The <u>old</u> computer, which had seen <u>ten</u> years of <u>loyal</u> service to its owner, finally malfunctioned in a <u>final</u> display of <u>bright</u> shocks and <u>loud</u> noises, indicating its end.

Drill 3 and Drill 4

1. <u>Those</u> directions will bring you to the wrong location; try <u>these</u> instead.
2. <u>This</u> phone has no service.
3. My favorite possession and the defining aspect of my life is <u>that</u> car: a 1999 Toyota Camry.
4. <u>This</u> company will not tolerate <u>this</u> type of reckless behavior, Mr. O'Sullivan.
5. <u>Those</u> buffoons just injured themselves while trying to use homemade fireworks.

"The moon shone <u>bright</u>; a sprinkling of snow covered the ground, and I reflected that she might, possibly, have taken it into her head to walk about the garden, for refreshment. I did detect a figure <u>creeping</u> along the <u>inner</u> fence of the park; but it was not my <u>young</u> mistress: on its emerging into the light, I recognized one of the grooms. He stood a <u>considerable</u> period, viewing the carriage-road through the grounds; then started off at a <u>brisk</u> pace, as if he had detected something, and reappeared presently, leading Miss's pony; and there she was, just <u>dismounted</u>. The man took his charge stealthily across the grass towards the stable. Cathy entered by the <u>casement</u> window of the <u>drawing</u> room and glided noiselessly up to where I awaited her. She put the door gently to, slipped off her <u>snowy</u> shoes, untied her hat, and was proceeding, <u>unconscious</u> of my espionage, to lay aside her mantle, when I suddenly rose and revealed myself."

VI. Adverbs

The tortoise plods slowly and the hare dashes quickly.

Adverbs answer the questions how, where, when, why, and to what extent. They modify verbs, adjectives, and other adjectives.

A. Adverbs that answer the questions how and to what extent

   Examples:
   - The choir is singing beautifully.

     (The adverb *beautifully* answers: how?)
   - We swam very quickly.

     (The adverb *very* answers: to what extent?)

     (The adverb *quickly* answers: how?)

B. Adverbs that answer the questions where and when

   Adverbs also answer where? and when? Sometimes, a noun can act as an adverb and answer the same questions adverbs answer.

   Examples:
   - I will finish my project tomorrow.

     (*Tomorrow* is a noun used as an adverb that modifies the verb *finish*.)

     (The adverb *tomorrow* answers: when?)
   - We can go home.

     (The verb *go* is modified by *home*, which is a noun used as an adverb.)

     (The adverb *home* answers: where?)

Drill 1 *Underline the adverbs in the following sentences, identify what question is answered by each adverb, and identify what word is modified by each adverb.*

How (H), When (WH), Where (WR), To What Extent (TWE)

1. Adam walked stealthily across the capture-the-flag field.

2. Hilary waved shyly at Josh as he called her name.

3. Josephina, who was very upset with Nathan, kicked him.

4. Thomas made his parents dinner yesterday.

5. Brian loves Rita intensely.

6. Peter is an exceedingly attractive man.

7. Bridget is not studying math.

8. Abby acted well in her school play.

9. Amy always wears flip-flops.

10. Clearly upset, Nina ran home crying.

11. Jill is taking the SAT tomorrow.

Answers on page 51

ANSWER KEY

Drill 1

1. Adam walked stealthily across the capture-the-flag field. **H**

2. Hilary waved shyly at Josh as he called her name. **H**

3. Josephine, who was very upset with Nathan, kicked him. **TWE**

4. Thomas made his parents dinner yesterday. **WH**

5. Brian loves Rita intensely. **H**

6. Peter is an exceedingly attractive man. **TWE**

7. Bridget is not studying math. **TWE**

8. Abby acted well in her school play. **H**

9. Amy always wears flip-flops. **TWE**

10. Clearly upset, Nina ran home crying. **H**

11. Jill is taking the SAT tomorrow. **WH**

VII. Prepositions

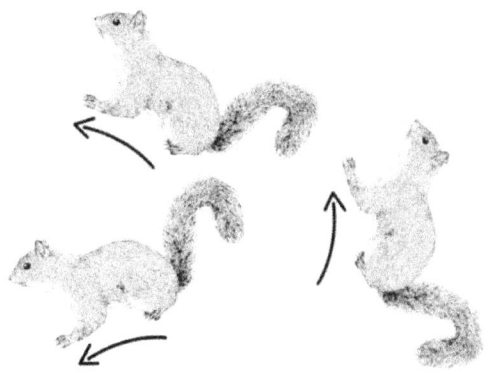

Everywhere a squirrel would go

Prepositional phrases provide additional information about a noun or a verb and show location, position, duration, possession, and more.

A. Prepositional Phrases

There are two kinds of prepositional phrases:

- **Adverbial** prepositional phrases: how, where, when, why, to what extent
- **Adjectival** prepositional phrases: what kind of

B. Commonly Used Prepositions

about	toward	until	upon
below	after	amid	at
for	besides	but	down
throughout	into	off	past
above	under	unto	with
beneath	against	among	before
from	between	by	during
to	like	on	since
across	underneath	up	within
beside	along	around	behind
in	beyond	concerning	except

Drill 1

In the following passage excerpted from Herman Melville's Moby Dick, *underline all 26 prepositions and bracket the prepositional phrases. Identify what each preposition modifies.*

"It was quite late in the evening when the little Moss came snugly to anchor, and Queequeg and I went ashore; so we could attend to no business that day, at least none but a supper and a bed. The landlord of the Spouter Inn had recommended us to his cousin Hosea Hussey of the Try Pots, whom he asserted to be the proprietor of one of the best kept hotels in all Nantucket, and moreover he had assured us that Cousin Hosea, as he called him, was famous for his chowders. In short, he plainly hinted that we could not possibly do better than try potluck at the Try Pots. But the directions he had given us about keeping a yellow warehouse on our starboard hand till we opened a white church to the larboard, and then keeping that on the larboard hand till we made a corner three points to the starboard, and that done, then ask the first man we met where the place was: these crooked directions of his very much puzzled us at first, especially as, at the outset, Queequeg insisted that the yellow warehouse—our first point of departure—must be left on the larboard hand, whereas I had understood Peter Coffin to say it was on the starboard."

ANSWER KEY

Drill 1

Some lines have been adjusted in order to demonstrate answers.

"It was quite late [in the evening] when the little Moss came snugly [to anchor], and Queequeg and I went ashore; so we could attend [to no business] that day, at least none [but a supper and a bed]. The landlord [of the Spouter Inn] had recommended us [to his cousin Hosea Hussey] [of the Try Pots], whom he asserted to be the proprietor [of one] [of the best kept hotels] [in all Nantucket], and moreover he had assured us that Cousin Hosea, as he called him, was famous [for his chowders]. [In short], he plainly hinted that we could not possibly do better than try potluck [at the Try Pots]. But the directions he had given us [about keeping a yellow warehouse] [on our starboard hand] till we opened a white church [to the larboard], and then keeping that [on the larboard hand] till we made a corner three points [to the starboard], and that done, then ask the first man we met where the place was: these crooked directions [of his] very much puzzled us [at first], especially as, [at the outset], Queequeg insisted that the yellow warehouse--our first point [of departure]--must be left [on the larboard hand], whereas I had understood Peter Coffin to say it was [on the starboard]."

VIII. Conjunctions

"I never saw a Moor--
I never saw the Sea--
Yet know I how the Heather looks
And what a Billow be.

I never spoke with God
Nor visited in Heaven--
Yet certain am I of the spot
As if the Chart were given--"

-Chartless, by Emily Dickinson

"And"   "Yet"

Conjunction junction what's your function?

"and"   "but"   "or"   "yet"

Conjunctions are used to join words or phrases together, while indicating their relationship.

A. Types of Conjunctions

Coordinating
- for, and, not, but, or, yet
    - *He trained for months, <u>but</u> he was not prepared to become a Marine.*
    - *Michael Collins won independence for much of Ireland, <u>yet</u> many Irishmen hated him.*

Correlative
- both… and, whether… or, not only… but also, either… or
    - *<u>Neither</u> the parents <u>nor</u> the students approved of the new teacher.*
    - *<u>Both</u> Eliza <u>and</u> her sister are cheerleaders.*

Subordinating
- because, although, while, since
    - *She had to file for bankruptcy <u>because</u> her savings were depleted.*
    - *The economy will not see a resurgence <u>unless</u> taxes decrease.*

Drill 1 *Identify the type of conjunctions used in each of the following sentences.*

Coordinating (COORD), Correlative (CORREL), Subordinating (SUB)

1. I cannot go to the party because I have more important commitments tonight.

2. Both law and medical school are extremely expensive.

3. Albert played basketball while his sister played tennis.

4. Neither the Prince nor the Queen have much influence over British politics.

5. Whether you decide to stay, or to leave, is your own decision.

6. The housing crisis of 2008 occurred because those with adjustable-rate mortgages couldn't handle the Fed's raising of interest rates.

7. Either Mike or Caleb has my keys.

8. Someone could graduate high school with a perfect GPA and SAT score yet still not qualify for Harvard University.

9. You are not allowed to go out or hang out with your friends tonight.

10. Although I find your business venture to be unique, I am not prepared to devote my own financial assets to your effort.

ANSWER KEY

Drill 1

1. I cannot go to the party because (SUB) I have more important commitments tonight.

2. Both (CORREL) law and medical school are extremely expensive.

3. Albert played basketball while (SUB) his sister played tennis.

4. Neither (CORREL) the Prince nor the Queen have much influence over British politics.

5. Whether (CORREL) you decide to stay, or to leave, is your own decision.

6. The housing crisis of 2008 occurred because (SUB) those with adjustable-rate mortgages couldn't handle the Fed's raising of interest rates.

7. Either (CORREL) Mike or Caleb has my keys.

8. Someone could graduate high school with a perfect GPA and SAT score yet (COORD) still not qualify for Harvard University.

9. You are not allowed to go out or (COORD) hang out with your friends tonight.

10. Although (SUB) I find your business venture to be unique, I am not prepared to devote my own financial assets to your effort.

IX. Interjections

"'But it's no use now,' thought poor Alice, "to pretend to be two people! Why, there's hardly enough of me left to make one respectable person!"

An interjection is a word used to express emotion or intense feeling. Interjections stand alone.

"**Why**, there's hardly…"

A. Commonly Used Interjections

Hooray	Ouch	Yuck
Oh	What	Gosh darn it
Alas	Holy smokes	Alas
Hey	Awesome	Yikes
Really	Oh	Help

Example: **Hey!** Do you want to come to the mall with us?

Structure Continued

*The Building Blocks of the Complex Sentence
Phrases and Clauses*

Phrases

*A **phrase** is a group of connected words that does not contain a subject and a verb.*

I. Prepositional Phrases

A ***preposition*** is everywhere a squirrel would go: *on* the table, *over* the table, *underneath* the table, *toward* the table.

Prepositional phrases are phrases that begin with a preposition and can function as adjectival or adverbial.

A. Adjectival Prepositional Phrases

Adjectival prepositional phrases connect nouns and pronouns to other words in the sentence and function as adjectives when they provide us with additional information about a noun to *show* its location, position, duration, or possession, and indicate what kind of noun it is or which noun it is. Such a phrase that describes a noun is adjectival.

Diagrams (the adjectival prepositional phrases are in brackets; the prepositions are in italics):

The man [*from* the shop] sold bicycles. (from the shop tells us which man)

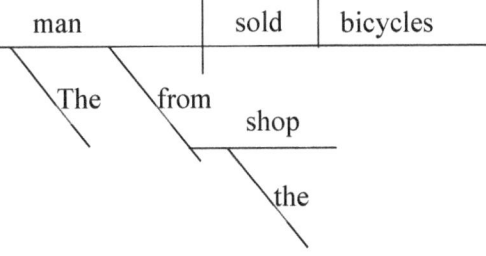

Asia is a continent [*with* many natural resources]. (with natural resources tells us which kind of continent)

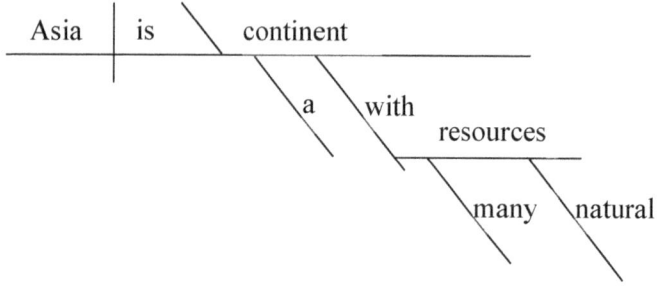

B. Adverbial Prepositional Phrases

Adverbial prepositional phrases *answer questions about how, where, when, why, and to what extent and function as adverbs.*

Diagrams (the adjectival prepositional phrases are in brackets; the prepositions are in italics):

The boy lifted the dirt [*with* a shovel]. (*with a shovel* tells how the boy lifted the dirt)

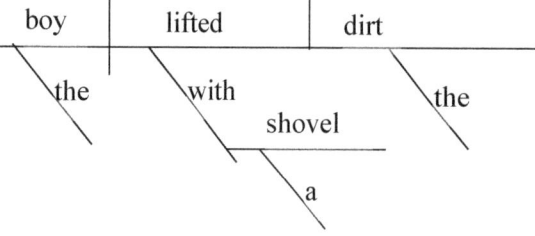

A herd of elephants rampaged [*through* the plains]. (*through the plains* tells where the herd of elephant rampaged)

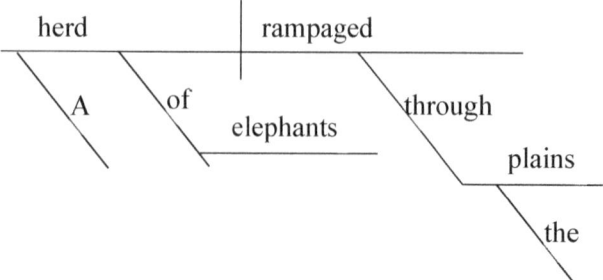

II. Verbals

A verbal is a form of a verb that takes a role in the sentence as another part of speech: an adjective, an adverb, or a noun. There are three types of verbals: participles, gerunds, and infinitives.

A. Participles

Participles are verbal adjectives. They demonstrate action while describing a subject. Participles can have both **past** and **present** tenses but can also form **participial phrases** with multiple words.

Present Participle	My mind is like a *racing* car.
Past Participle	The *broken* playset rested on the floor.
Participial Phrase	*Sensing the need for action*, James Bond saved the Prime Minister.

Diagrams: I want a *working* cell phone. (*working* is a present participle that describes what kind of phone)

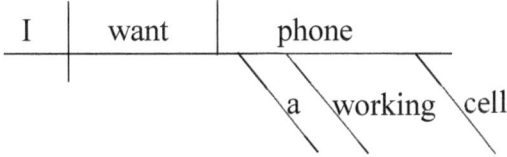

The *crying* boy has a *broken* ankle. (*crying* is a present participle that describes boy, and *broken* is a past participle that describes ankle)

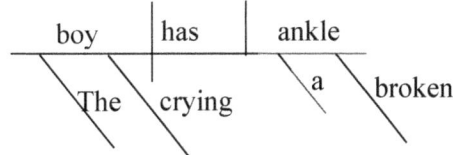

B. Gerunds

Gerunds are verbal nouns. They are created by adding *-ing* to the present tense of verbs. Gerunds can serve as the subject, direct object, indirect object, predicate nominative, appositive, or object of a preposition. It is easy to confuse gerunds with present progressive verbs because both end in *-ing*.

Subject   *Driving* is my favorite activity.
Direct Object   I prefer *swimming as a sport.*
Indirect Object   I give *working* much of my time.
Predicate Nominative   My favorite activity is *driving.*
Appositive   My favorite activity, *observing birds in the park*, is a fun diversion.
Object of Preposition After *feeding the birds in the park*, I am happy.

Present Progressive Verbs (NOT GERUNDS): She *is running*. He *is smiling*.

Diagrams: *Reading* is fun   → functions as a noun answering the question what is fun

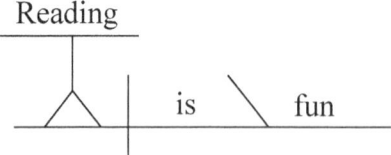

Sam hates *fighting.*   → functions as a noun and is the direct object of hates

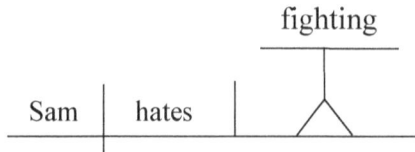

C. Infinitives

Infinitives are created with *to* plus the present tense of a verb: *to go, to see, to know,* etc. Infinitives can combine with their objects and modifiers to create infinitive phrases. Infinitives and infinitive phrases can serve as adjectives, adverbs, or nouns.

Adjective   The poster says that this dealership has trucks *to sell to customers.*
Adverb   The inmates hurried *to see the fight.*
Noun:

    Subject   *To waste time* is irritating.

    Direct Object   High schoolers like *to experience* a sense of individuality.

    Predicate Nominative   My aspiration is *to win the championship.*

    Object of Preposition   We demand nothing except *to be free.*

    Appositive   Jared's final chore, *to clean his room,* was finished.

Diagrams: Do you have a form *to fill?* → functions as an adjective that describes the direct object form.

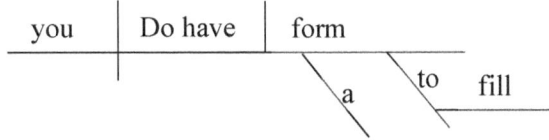

The tiny font in the textbook was hard *to read.* → functions as an adverb answering the question *how?*

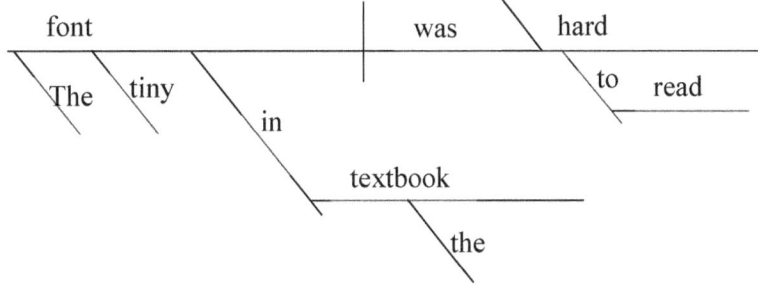

Clauses

A *clause* is a group of words containing a subject and a verb. **Dependent clauses** can function as adjectives, adverbs, or nouns. Throughout this unit, we will work with dependent clauses, sometimes also called subordinate clauses. Independent clauses will not appear until the unit on run-on sentences.

I. Adjectival Clauses

Adjectival clauses usually begin with a relative pronoun, which connects the dependent clause to a noun or pronoun. Some adjectival clauses, however, can begin with relative adverbs such as when, where, and why. Adjectival clauses modify nouns or pronouns.

Relative pronoun: who, whom, whose, that, which

Relative adverbs: when, where, why

Diagrams:
I went to her house, where she lives.

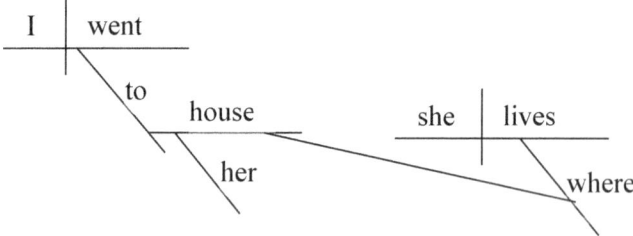

Mary has a sister who goes to college.

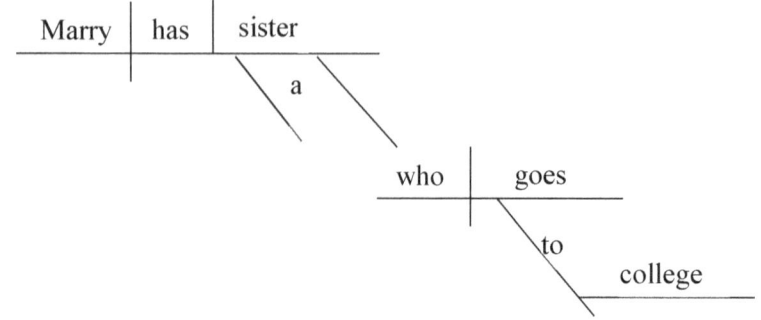

II. Adverbial Clauses

Adverbial clauses begin with a coordinating conjunction and can modify a verb, adjective, or another adverb. Coordinating conjunctions can include indications of concession, condition, comparison, time, place, reason, or manner.

Condition (if)   if, unless, provided that, in case
Comparison (to what extent)   than, whether, whereas, as much as
Time (when)   when, whenever, anywhere, until
Place (where)   where, wherever, anywhere, everywhere
Reason (why)   because, since, so that, why
Manner (how)   how, as though, as if
Concession (to what extent / how)   although, though, even though, while

Diagram:

I will fail this test if I do not study.

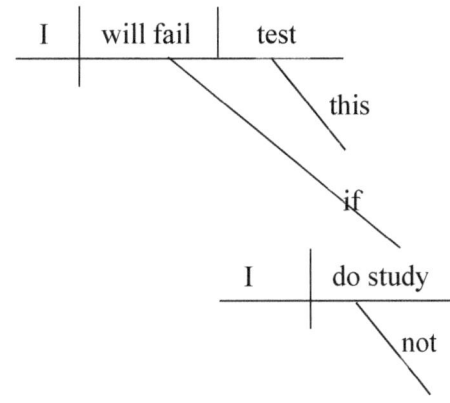

III. Noun Clauses

Noun clauses begin with a relative pronoun and can act as *a subject, direct subject, object of a preposition, predicate nominative, or appositive.*

Different Types - subject, predicate nominative, direct object, appositive, object of preposition

Subject	What he sees in the dark is a ghost.
Predicate Nominative	The pay raise is what the employee wants.
Direct Object	I can't tell you what Mr. White did.
Appositive	The fact that we are together gives me hope.
Object of Preposition	I understand nothing about the problem except what NPR said.

Relative Pronoun - who, whom, what, that, whatever, whoever, whomever

Who	I can't see *who just arrived at the party.*
Whom	Prince Charming searched desperately to find *whom the slipper belonged to.*
What	*What the professor said* was intelligent.
That	She noticed *that he had an orange hat.*
Whatever	I will tell him *whatever he needs to know.*
Whoever	We can expel *whoever doesn't respect our policies.*
Whomever	You can give the job to *whomever you want.*

Relative Adverb - when, where, why, how

When	It is important to know *when to save money.*
Where	We need raincoats for *where we are going.*
Why	I remember *why you transferred schools.*
How	I often think about *how moral humans really are.*

Diagram:

What my sister said was not very polite.

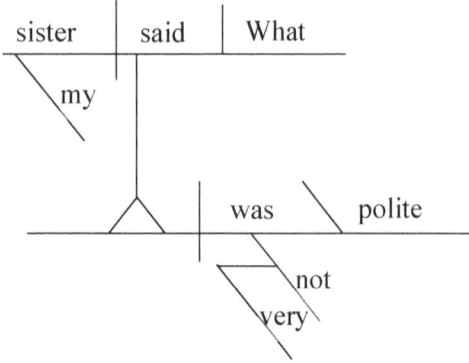

67

GRAMMAR

The rules one must master to write proper sentences: nouns and pronouns, their cases and number; verbs, their tenses and mood; adjectives and adverbs, their proper placements; conjunctions, their balance of words before and after. Rules govern how thoughts are made understandable, shared by everyone using the language: speaker or listener, writer or reader.

Problems with Verbs

Diagnostic Test

Determine if the sentence is grammatically correct. Correct all errors.

1. I am enjoying my time in California, but I sometimes wish that I was home with my family.

2. Floating in the pool. the rubber duck looked as if it was chewed by a wild animal.

3. Galileo was put on trial for stating that the sun was the center of the galaxy.

4. Did you clean the dishes and take out the trash yet?

5. Over many years, I studied how to paint like Picasso, but I still have a lot to learn.

6. Stephen Hawking discovered that there are situations where Einstein's equations break down.

7. If I were in San Francisco, I would go to tonight's San Francisco Giants game at AT&T Park.

8. After the birthday boy opened his door, we all jumped out of our hiding spots to wish him a happy birthday.

9. Already my brother has promised not only to come to my concert but also to invite his wife, Janet.

10. I am not finished, but I will finish soon.

Problems with Verbs

This chapter covers the most common mistakes that can arise with the use of verbs.

In simplest terms, a sentence consists of a subject—a noun or pronoun, which is a person, place, or thing— and a predicate—its verb, which shows an action like "run," "grab," or "enact" or a state of being like "is," "appears," or "seems."

I. Verb Tenses

As mentioned in earlier chapters, ***verb tenses*** describe when an action is happening, was happening, or will be happening.

Tense:	*Examples:*
Present	<ul><li>I love running in the park.</li><li>He studies every school night.</li><li>The President delivers his State of the Union address at 7 p.m.</li></ul>
Past	<ul><li>I gained admission to Harvard Law School yesterday.</li><li>She served in the Marines for five years.</li></ul>
Future	<ul><li>I will submit the grievances this upcoming week.</li><li>If the tenant decides to withdraw prematurely from the leasing contract, she will lose five thousand dollars.</li></ul>
Present Progressive **Past Progressive** **Future Progressive**	<ul><li>I am working.</li><li>I was working.</li><li>I will be working.</li></ul>

II. Verb Mood

The mood of a verb denotes the attitude that the speaker assumes toward the verb's action. The most common mood, the indicative, describes an action that is regarded as undisputed fact or truth. It is important to realize that the action does not have to be true in real life, only regarded as true in the sentence.

A. Indicative

The indicative mood is used for action that is regarded as undisputed fact or truth.

Examples:

- Murder is a capital offense.
- The pig flew over Italy. (Although this sentence is not true, notice how the verb asserts the fact as truth. If the sentence had read "The pig might have flown over Italy," then the verb would not be indicative.)

B. Subjunctive

The subjunctive mood is used for action that may be uncertain, hoped for, disputable, dependent on another action or condition, or simply contrary to fact.

Examples:

- If I were in Paris right now, I would visit the Eiffel Tower.
- Thomas Edison might have stolen many of Nikola Tesla's ideas.
- If it had snowed yesterday, I would have made a snowman.

C. Imperative

The imperative mood is used for action that is issued as a command.

Examples:

- Rachael, fetch me the axe.
- Don't sit on my bed!

III. For Permanent Truths, Use Present Tense

Things that are always true always use present tense.

Present tense expresses actions that are currently happening.

Examples: I am.
You are.
We are.

Examples:

    Correct: Scientists discovered that water *boils* at 100°C.
    Incorrect: Scientists discovered that water *boiled* at 100°C.

    Correct: Christopher Columbus believed that the Earth *is* round.
    Incorrect: Christopher Columbus believed that the Earth *was* round.

IV. Double Negatives

Double negatives make a sentence unclear and illogical and are placed here as a subset of "Problems with Verbs."

Diagnostic Test

Determine if the sentence is grammatically correct. Correct all errors.

1. I couldn't scarcely tell what was going on in my own house.

2. It is not too late to do anything to fix the problem now, I don't think.

3. I have no doubt but that my score on the math test would have been higher if I hadn't spent the past night watching cartoons until 3:23 a.m.

4. Without hardly any money left in the bank, the man wondered how he would pay his rent that was due on Saturday.

5. I could not think of a reason why I wouldn't attend my daughter's piano recital.

6. I didn't believe George when he said that he wouldn't attend his mother's funeral.

7. I did not say nothing to Tom; I have no idea how he found out our little secret.

8. Despite opposition from the business community, the politician refused to promise that he wouldn't effect a new business tax.

9. I could not hardly understand my professor who spent most of his life in France and had a strong French accent.

10. I expect you to have neither enough money to buy a Super Bowl ring nor enough talent to win a Super Bowl.

Note: **Double negatives** raise logical contradictions with verbs.

A. *A **double negative** occurs when two or more negative words are used together to describe the same thing.*

Examples: Double Negative: I will *not* tell *nobody*.

Double Negative: I am *not* going to give money to *no-one*.

Double negatives are confusing and should be avoided, because they cancel each other out.

Examples: *I will not tell nobody* means *I will tell somebody*.

I am not going to give money to no-one means *I am going to give money to someone*.

B. Common negative words

aren't	can't	couldn't	didn't	haven't	isn't	isn't	neither	never
no	no one	nobody	none	not	nothing	nowhere	wasn't	weren't

C. Barely, Scarcely, Hardly

Barely, *scarcely*, *hardly*, and their synonyms are also negative words. Don't combine these words with another negative word to describe the same thing.

Examples: Double Negative: I *don't barely* have enough motivation to get out of bed.

Double Negative: I want to go to the beach, but there is *not scarcely* enough time left in the day.

Double Negatives Exercises

Determine if the sentence is grammatically correct. Correct all errors.

1. I have no doubt, my tutor says, but that learning grammar is vital to my success.

2. I love my friend, George, but his poor attitude will get him nowhere.

3. I acknowledge that I can't help, regardless of my desire to become a better role model to my daughter, succumbing to my urge to smoke cigarettes—I don't think.

4. Without hardly any reason to stay in Orlando, Florida, I moved back to my hometown in Columbus, Ohio.

5. There is not, the restaurant employee told me, scarcely a wait for food on Saturday nights.

6. I believe that people can't survive without food and water.

7. I could not scarcely muster enough courage to ask my crush out to the school dance.

8. I have no doubts but that my friend will become a successful entrepreneur.

9. I can't even begin to comprehend the difficulties that my mother faced: running away from the mafia and then lacking money to buy daily necessities.

10. I wouldn't be able to live without enough money to pay my bills.

Problems with Verbs Exercises

Determine if the sentence is grammatically correct. Correct all errors.

1. If I was a little bit faster, I would be faster than you are.

2. I have been working on this project for the past seven years, but I am hoping to finish tomorrow.

3. I am enjoying your party, but I wish my best friend, Samantha, were here.

4. If you have already finished your dinner, then you can have dessert.

5. Isaac Newton believed that gravity caused the planets to orbit the Sun.

6. I told my brother that I finally learned how to use our dishwasher.

7. My mother wishes that I decided to go to college in California, but I enjoyed my first semester in Hawaii.

8. The killer testified that in all of his life he never thought of himself as the bad guy.

9. Despite the fact that she didn't finish her chores yet, the girl snuck off to play basketball.

10. For the first thirty years of my life, I never saw a tiger.

11. After the fraternity brothers drunk enough whiskey, they began to haze and humiliate the new freshman pledges who had just joined the house.

12. If the principal would have consulted the school committee before presenting the controversial budget, the heated argument over expenditures would have never happened.

13. If I was the chairperson of the history department, I would constantly be in contact with students and faculty alike.

14. To have tunneled successfully through the concrete prison walls, Andy Dufresne would have to begin his escaping scheme upon his arrival to Shawshank State Penitentiary.

15. Christopher Columbus believed that the Earth was round.

16. I have already gone to Rockport several times this year.

17. Congress has not passed the bill yet because they have in vain been wishing it were a problem for the courts to solve.

18. Did you finish your homework yet?

19. Every day, the professor reminds the students in his lectures that Rome was the capital of the most extensive empire known to man.

20. The fisherman is hoping to have brought in his catch of the day before last evening had turned to dawn.

Answers

Problems with Verbs Diagnostic

1. Grammatically Incorrect. Corrected: I am enjoying my time in California, but I sometimes wish that I **were** home with my family.
2. Grammatically Incorrect. Corrected: Floating in the pool. the rubber duck looked as if it **had been** chewed by a wild animal.
3. Grammatically Incorrect. Corrected: Galileo was put on trial for stating that the sun **is** the center of the galaxy.
4. Grammatically Incorrect. Corrected: **Have** you **cleaned** the dishes and **taken** out the trash yet?
5. Grammatically Incorrect. Corrected: Over many years, I **have** studied how to paint like Picasso, but I still have a lot to learn.
6. Grammatically Correct
7. Grammatically Correct
8. Grammatically Incorrect. Corrected: After the birthday boy **had opened** his door, we all jumped out of our hiding spots to wish him a happy birthday.
9. Grammatically Correct
10. Grammatically Incorrect. Corrected: I **have** not finished, but I will finish soon.

Double Negatives Diagnostic

1. Not grammatically correct. There is a double negative. Corrected: I could scarcely tell what was going on in my own house.
2. Not grammatically correct. There is a double negative. Corrected: It is not too late to do anything to fix the problem now.
3. Not grammatically correct. There is a double negative. Corrected: I have no doubt that my score on the math test would have been higher if I hadn't spent the past night watching cartoons until 3:23 a.m.
4. Not grammatically correct. There is a double negative. Corrected: With hardly any money left in the bank, the man wondered how he would pay his rent that was due on Saturday.
5. Grammatically correct.
6. Grammatically correct.
7. Not grammatically correct. There is a double negative. Corrected: I did not say anything to Tom; I have no idea how he found out our little secret.
8. Grammatically correct.
9. Not grammatically correct. There is a double negative. Corrected: I could hardly understand my professor who spent most of his life in France and had a strong French accent.
10. Grammatically correct.

Double Negative Exercises

1. Not grammatically correct. There is a double negative. Corrected: I have no doubt, my tutor says, that learning grammar is vital to my success.

2. Grammatically correct
3. Not grammatically correct. There is a double negative. Corrected: I acknowledge that I can't help, regardless of my desire to become a better role model to my daughter, succumbing to my urge to smoke cigarettes.
4. Not grammatically correct. There is a double negative. Corrected: With hardly any reason to stay in Orlando, Florida, I moved back to my hometown in Columbus, Ohio.
5. Not grammatically correct. There is a double negative. Corrected: There is, the restaurant employee told me, scarcely a wait for food on Saturday nights.
6. Grammatically correct
7. Not grammatically correct. There is a double negative. I could scarcely muster enough courage to ask my crush out to the school dance.
8. Not grammatically correct. There is a double negative. I have no doubts that my friend will become a successful entrepreneur.
9. Grammatically correct
10. Grammatically correct

Problems with Verbs Exercises

1. Grammatically Incorrect. Corrected: If I **were** a little bit faster, I would be faster than you are.
2. Grammatically Correct
3. Grammatically Correct
4. Grammatically Correct
5. Grammatically Incorrect. Corrected: Isaac Newton believed that gravity **causes** the planets to orbit the Sun.
6. Grammatically Incorrect. Corrected: I told my brother that I **had** finally learned how to use our dishwasher.
7. Grammatically Incorrect. Corrected: My mother wishes that I **had** decided to go to college in California, but I enjoyed my first semester in Hawaii.
8. Grammatically Incorrect. Corrected: The killer testified that in all of his life he **had** never thought of himself as the bad guy.
9. Grammatically Incorrect. Corrected: Despite the fact that she **hadn't finished** her chores yet, the girl snuck off to play basketball.
10. Grammatically Incorrect. Corrected: For the first thirty years of my life, I **had** never **seen** a tiger.
11. Grammatically Incorrect. Corrected: After the fraternity brothers had drunk enough whiskey, they began to haze and humiliate the new freshman pledges who had just joined the house.
12. Grammatically Incorrect. Corrected: If the principal had consulted the school committee before presenting the controversial budget, the heated argument over expenditures never would have never happened.
13. Grammatically Incorrect. Corrected: If I were the chairperson of the history department, I would constantly be in contact with students and faculty alike.

14. Grammatically Incorrect. Corrected: To have tunneled successfully through the concrete prison walls, Andy Dufresne would have had to begin his escaping scheme upon his arrival to Shawshank State Penitentiary.
15. Grammatically Incorrect. Corrected: Christopher Columbus believed that the Earth is round.
16. Grammatically Correct.
17. Grammatically Correct.
18. Grammatically Incorrect. Corrected: Have you finished your homework yet?
19. Grammatically Correct.
20. Grammatically Incorrect. Corrected: The fisherman was hoping to have brought in his catch of the day before last evening had turned to dawn.

Subject-Verb Agreement

Diagnostic Test

Select the letter of the correct choice and circle the noun or nouns that determine whether the verb's subject is singular or plural. The answers are at the end of the unit.

1. Running for an hour and then jumping for another hour (A. is B. are) my favorite exercise routine.

2. Surprisingly, none of the nuclei (A. was B. were) damaged during the earthquake, which measured 5.8 on the Richter scale.

3. The senator along with her assistants (A. is B. are) planning to attend the peaceful protest.

4. Eight miles (A. is B. are) the farthest that I've ever run.

5. Neither the cheerleaders nor their coach (A. is B. are) happy about the football team's loss last night.

6. The admissions office told me that there (A. is B. are) a large number of students who get good grades.

7. Jake is one of the athletes who (A. is B. are) very superstitious.

8. *Breaking Bad* is one of the best shows that (A. happens B. happen) to be set in New Mexico.

9. There (A. is B. are) a lot of empty bottles strewn across the otherwise pristine beach.

10. The quality of crops in the region (A. is B. are) poor because of the lack of nitrogen in the soil.

Subject-Verb Agreement

I. Singular Subjects Needs Singular Verbs, Plural Subjects Need Plural Verbs

In a clear and logical English sentence, the *number*, which can be singular or plural, of a verb must match the *number* of its subject, the "who" or "what" that does the action of the verb.

Examples: She eats. (singular subject and singular verb)

They eat. (plural subject and plural verb)

A lack of pencils precludes students from taking notes.

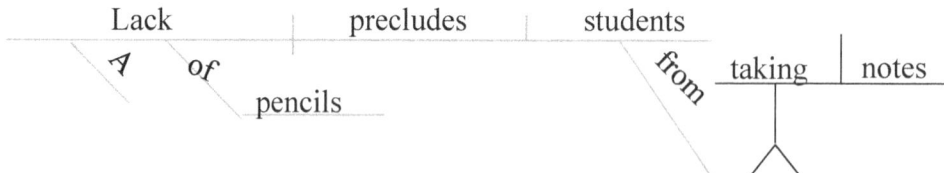

Note that the subject of the verb is not always obvious. In the above example, the subject of the verb to preclude is "lack." The pencils don't preclude students from taking notes. The lack of pencils is what precludes students from taking notes.

It is not always apparent whether subjects are singular or plural. The background information that follows is needed to understand how to determine whether the subject agrees with the verb.

II. Phrases and Clauses in between the Subject and Verb

A verb can be separated from its subject by phrases or clauses. In this case, the subject can be found by removing an entire phrase or dependent clause. Notice the following examples.

- Kelly, the woman painting my nails, is telling me a story about gardening.

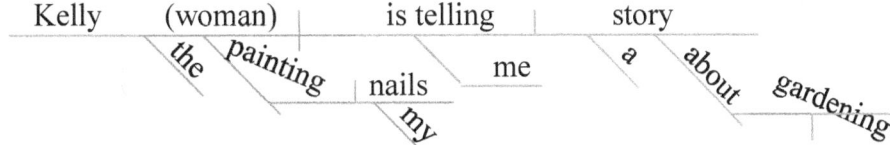

The woman painting my nails is a phrase that modifies Kelly by helping to identify who she is. After removing this phrase, the remaining sentence is *Kelly is telling me a story about gardening*. Therefore, Kelly is the singular subject of the verb to be.

- The state senator, a former businessman who started four companies, is running for re-election.

The state senator is modified by the phrase *a former businessman who started four companies*. After removing this phrase, the remaining sentence is *The state senator is running for re-election*. Therefore, senator is the singular subject of the verb to be.

- Cars that get great gas mileage are better for the environment.

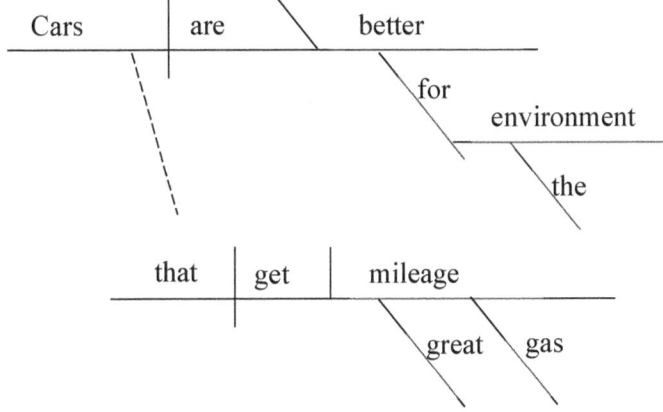

Cars is modified by the clause *that get great gas mileage*. After removing this clause, the remaining sentence is *Cars are better for the environment*. Therefore, cars is the plural subject of the verb are.

III. Verbs in a Clause

A verb that is inside a subordinate clause will have a subject from the same clause. Notice the following examples.

- Mike is one of those students who never study enough.

Study is part of the subordinate clause *who never study enough*. *Who* is the subject of the verb to study. *Who* stands in for the *students*, and so the subject *who* is plural. *Mike* is not the subject, because *Mike* is part of the main clause and not the subordinate clause.

- The number of Americans who understand Latin is declining.

Understand is part of the subordinate clause *who understand Latin*. *Who* is the subject of the verb to understand. *Who* stands in for *Americans*, and so the subject *who* is plural. Notice that the subject of *is declining* is *the number*, which is possible because they are both part of the main clause.

- My watch is one of those that easily break.

Break is part of the subordinate clause *that easily break*. *That* is the subject of the verb to break. *That* stands in for *those*, and so the subject *that* is plural.

Drill 1 *Circle the letter of the correct choice.*
1. Jane is one of those girls who (A. eats B. eat) snacks all day long.
2. The cars that I bought at a charity auction (A. was B. were) very affordable.
3. The temperature, which can be measured by thermometers, (A. is B. are) 34 degrees= Fahrenheit.
4. Her sisters, who happen to be over six feet tall, (A. is B. are) happy.
5. Jasmine is one of the baseball players who (A. prefers B. prefer) to use batting gloves.
6. The lack of Americans who (A. knows B. know) how to program hurts our economy.

IV. Verb Before its Subject

A verb can come before its subject. Notice the following examples where the subject is in italics.

- Here are many *examples* of subject-verb agreement. (the subject is *examples* because it is the examples that are here)
- Inside the walls lives a *rat*. (the subject is *rat* because it is the rat that lives inside the walls)
- Here are *a pencil and a pen* on the table. (the subject is *a pencil and a pen* because it is the pencil and the pen that are on the table)
- Does *Mary* like Peter? (the subject is *Mary* because it is Mary who does or doesn't like Peter)

Mary	Does like	Peter

Drill 2 *Circle the letter of the correct choice.*
1. How (A. was B. were) your vacation in the southwest and northwest parts of France?
2. There (A. is B. are) many reasons to go to college.
3. On top of the mountain (A. lives B. live) a flock of goats.
4. Here (A. is B. are) the pen and pad you need to keep notes.
5. In this town, there (A. is B. are) a police station and a library.
6. (A. Do B. Does) the president and vice president agree to the terms?

V. Three Types of And

There are two cases where "and" appears within a subject but the subject remains singular.

If "and" is used to mean plus as in four and three, the subject will be singular.
- Eight and seven is fifteen. (and is used to mean plus)

If "and" is used to express a single cohesive unit, the subject will be singular.
- Ham and eggs is the best item on their menu. (Ham and eggs is a single dish on the menu)
- Hide and seek is my favorite game to play. (Hide and seek is a single game)

Otherwise, the subject is plural.
- Ham and eggs are the last two foods on my shopping list. (Two different foods)
- Bingo and Yahtzee are my least favorite games to play. (Two different games)

VI. Along with, as well as, in addition to

If the subject is two things combined using "along with", "as well as", "in addition to" or another preposition, then the subject's number is equal to the number of what comes before the preposition

- The coach *along with the cheerleaders* is planning to attend the movie premiere.
- Bernie Sanders *as well as all of the Democratic senators* plans to vote to approve the bill.
- A small bonus *in addition to their regular pay* was given to the employees.

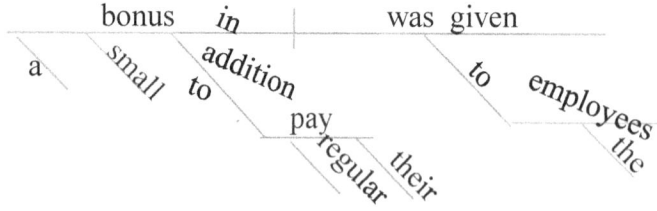

Drill 3 *Circle the letter of the correct choice.*
1. Batman as well as his sidekicks (A. fights B. fight) criminals.
2. Spring and summer (A. is B. are) my favorite seasons.
3. Nine and ten (A. is B. are) nineteen.
4. The cheerleaders along with the mascot (A. is B. are) currently performing.
5. Peanut butter and jelly (A. was B. were) Sam's favorite type of sandwich.
6. My work ethic along with my knowledge of the industry (A. makes B. make) me a good fit for your company.

VII. Either, neither

If "either" or "neither" is the subject, then the subject is singular.

- Either is affordable.
- Neither was to the food critic's liking.

VIII. Or, nor

If the subject is two things combined using "or", "nor", the subject's number is equal to the number of what comes after the conjunction.

- Jack or his friends are responsible for the prank.
- Either my friends or Jack is responsible for the prank.
- Neither my hunger nor my thirst is preventing me from completing this marathon.

IX. Not only, but also

If the subject is two things combined using "not only" and "but also," the subject's number is equal to the number of what comes after "but also."

- Not only regular exercise but also a healthy diet is beneficial to your health.
- Not only the cheerleaders but also the coach is planning to attend.
- Not only the coach but also the cheerleaders are planning to attend.

Drill 4 *Circle the letter of the correct choice.*
1. Either Jack or Jill (A. has B. have) rolled down the hill.
2. Not only chocolates but also cake (A. is B. are) available at the buffet.
3. Neither (A. wants B. want) to go to jail.
4. Jane or Jason (A. steals B. steal) from the candy store.
5. Either the candy or the ice cream (A. is B. are) delicious.
6. The screen or the teachers (A. informs B. inform) students of what to expect.

X. Each, every, one, body, thing

The following subjects are singular: anybody, anyone, anything, each, everybody, everyone, everything, nobody, no one, nothing, one, somebody, someone, something

- Everything happens for a reason.
- Everyone is expected to turn in his or her homework.
- Nobody wants to come to the game today.

A subject will be singular if it is modified by: each, every, one

- Each soccer player receives a trophy.

- Every one of the cheerleaders is unhappy.
- One of the socks is torn.

XI. Some of, all of, any of, half of

For *some of* something, the subject's number is the number of what comes after *some of*.

- Some of the icicles have melted. (Some of the icicles is plural because icicles is plural)
- Some of the cake was crushed during the delivery. (Some of the cake is singular because cake is singular)

Similarly, for *all of* or *any of* something, the subject's number is the number of what comes after all or any of.

- All of the snow has fallen. (All of the snow is singular because snow is singular)
- If any of the ingredients are missing, I can buy more at the store. (Any of the ingredients is plural because ingredients is plural)

Similarly, for *some percent* or *fraction (half, one-fourth, etc.) of* something, then the subject's number is the number of what comes after the percent or fraction.

- One-third of doctors recommend this product. (One third of doctors is plural because doctors is plural)
- Half of the bread is moldy. (Half of bread is singular because bread is singular)

Drill 5 *Circle the letter of the correct choice.*
1. One third of the boys (A. is B. are) sick.
2. Not one of the boys (A. is B. are) going to come.
3. Every single one of the cheerleaders (A. is B. are) happy.
4. Some of the cheerleaders (A. is B. are) happy.
5. Anybody who (A. shows B. show) up to the birthday party will receive a gift bag.
6. All of them (A. is B. are) capable of dunking a basketball.

XII. Collective nouns

A collective noun is a word that refers to a collection of things taken as a whole. Examples include ten minutes, family, committee, team, and jury. Though collective nouns are often singular, if the author wants to emphasize the individuals in the collectives, then the noun is plural.

- The jury is ready to announce its verdict. (The jury is acting together)
- The jury are about to return to their homes. (All of the individual members of the jury are returning home)
- The Kennedy family is in the Bahamas, where they are playing beach volleyball among themselves.

- The school committee were debating among themselves.
- The school committee has reached its verdict.
- The basketball team is playing its first game on Thursday.
- Ten miles is the distance between my house and your house. (Ten miles is a whole distance)

There are some exceptions, like sports team names. The full team name (i.e., Boston Red Sox) is plural, the organization (Red Sox organization) is singular, and the city name (i.e., Boston) is singular.
- The Boston Red Sox are playing today. (full team name is plural)
- The Red Sox organization is run very well. (organization is a cohesive unit, so it is singular)
- Boston is playing tomorrow (city name is singular)

XIII. Tricky nouns

Most plural nouns end in "s." There are, however, singular nouns that end in "s." These nouns normally represent a concept like statistics, gymnastics, news and politics.
- Gymnastics is a lot more difficult than I thought it would be.
- Physics is a branch of science.

There are also plural nouns that don't end in "s." Consider the following chart:

Singular	Plural
Alumnus	alumni
Bacterium	bacteria
Criterion	criteria
Curriculum	curricula
Die	dice
Fungus	fungi
Medium	media
memorandum	memoranda
sister-in-law	sisters-in-law
Nucleus	nuclei
Radius	radii
son-in-law	sons-in-law
Syllabus	syllabi

- The criteria for admittance include high grades. (*criteria* is plural)
- The dice were given to me by my grandmother. (*dice* is plural)
- My sons-in-law, Jack and John, are at the party. (*sons-in-law* is plural)
- The syllabi are posted on the school website. (*syllabi* is plural)

Drill 6 *Circle the letter of the correct choice.*
1. My criterion for accepting friend requests (A. has B. have) recently changed.

2. The herd (A. is B. are) running towards me.
3. The herd (A. is B. are) scattering.
4. The acceptance criteria (A. is B. are) located on our website.
5. Ten thousand dollars (A. was B. were) awarded to the plaintiff.
6. The dice (A. is B. are) brand new.

Subject-Verb Agreement Exercises

Select the letter of the correct choice and circle the noun or nouns that determine whether the verb's subject is singular or plural.

1. A large number of students (A. is B. are) attending the rally.
2. The number of students attending private school (A. is B. are) rising.
3. John as well as his friends (A. is B. are) planning to attend tonight's football game.
4. Either flavor (A. is B. are) a good choice.
5. (A. Do B. Does) either girl want dessert?
6. Neither Jack nor Jill (A. is B. are) going to attend the school play.
7. There (A. was B. were) a lot of fans at the game.
8. 30 minutes (A. is B. are) the average wait time at our restaurant.
9. The physics responsible for the balls' movements (A. is B. are) very complicated.
10. 10 dollars and 20 cents (A. is B. are) how much money I have in my pocket.
11. Every one of the cheerleaders (A. is B. are) happy.
12. My criteria for what makes a good car (A. is B. are) unique.
13. The jury (A. is B. are) ready to make a verdict.
14. The lack of water and nutrients (A. has B. have) made the Sahara Desert barren.
15. The United Arab Emirates (A. is B. are) a country in the Middle East.
16. Half of their army (A. is B. are) located at that base.
17. The bacteria (A. is B. are) not infectious.
18. Apple pie and ice cream (A. is B. are) my favorite dessert.
19. Apple pie and ice cream (A. is B. are) two of my favorite desserts.
20. My compass along with my sense of direction (A. is B. are) why I got home safely.
21. Four and three (A. is B. are) seven.
22. The Who (A. is B. are) one of the best bands of all time.
23. *The Walking Dead*, a popular TV show about zombies, (A. was B. were) nominated for an Emmy.
24. This sort of laughing and crying (A. is B. are) not too uncommon.
25. Half of the soldiers (A. is B. are) located at that base.

Subject-Verb Agreement Exercises

Select the letter of the correct choice and circle the noun or nouns that determine whether the verb's subject is singular or plural.

26. Neither one of them (A. is B. are) capable of dunking a basketball.
27. Nine out of ten doctors (A. recommends B. recommend) exercising at least once per day.
28. J.K. Rowling is among the authors who (A. has B. have) made over one million dollars.
29. The map left for the travelers (A. was B. were) very helpful.
30. The types of food that I like to eat (A. includes B. include) pasta.
31. The abundance of candy and chocolates (A. makes B. make) my grandmother's house appealing to children.
32. The dice (A. was B. were) pink.
33. At school today, I learned why studying past events (A. is B. are) so important.
34. The running and swimming that we did in gym class (A. was B. were) very tiring.
35. The football coach along with his family (A. is B. are) at the school play.
36. Drinking and driving (A. is B. are) against the law.
37. Drinking and driving (A. is B. are) amusing things to do, but they should never be done at the same time.
38. The scientist's theses (A. was B. were) highly regarded.
39. None of the cheerleaders (A. is B. are) happy.
40. Not one of the cheerleaders (A. is B. are) happy.
41. The Who (A. was B. were) some of the biggest celebrities in the 1970s.
42. There (A. is B. are) a number of chocolates inside the store.
43. All of the radii except for one (A. is B. are) five centimeters.
44. My parents, who were both born in Boston, (A. roots B. root) for the Red Sox.
45. The lack of students who read at a proficient level (A. is B. are) appalling.
46. The fungi on the table (A. is B. are) growing.
47. My ability to solve math problems (A. is B. are) not as strong as I want it to be.
48. Their running (A. is B. are) at a level superior to mine.
49. Gin and tonic (A. is B. are) my favorite drink.
50. The game where players run around in circles until they fall down (A. is B. are) really fun.

Subject - Verb Agreement Answers

Diagnostic

1. A   routine is
2. B   nuclei were
3. A   senator is
4. A   Eight miles is
5. A   coach is
6. B   students are
7. B   athletes are
8. B   shows happen
9. B   bottles are
10. A   quality is

Drill 1

1. B
2. B
3. A
4. B
5. B
6. B

Drill 2

1. A
2. B
3. A
4. B
5. B
6. A

Drill 3

1. A
2. B
3. A
4. B
5. A
6. A

Drill 4

1. A
2. A
3. A
4. A
5. A
6. B

Drill 5

1. B
2. A
3. A
4. B
5. A
6. B

Drill 6

1. A
2. A
3. B
4. B
5. A
6. B

Questions

1. B students are
2. A number is
3. A John is
4. A Either flavor is
5. B either girl does
6. A Jill is
7. B fans were
8. A 30 minutes is
9. A physics
10. A 10 dollars and 20 cents
11. A Everyone
12. B criteria are
13. A jury is
14. A lack has
15. A United Arab Emirates is
16. A army is
17. B bacteria are
18. A dessert is
19. B desserts are
20. A compass is
21. A Four and three is
22. A The Who is
23. A *The Walking Dead* was
24. A This sort is
25. B soldiers are
26. A Neither one is
27. B Nine doctors recommend
28. B authors have
29. A map was
30. B types include
31. A abundance makes
32. B dice were
33. A studying is
34. B running and swimming were
35. A coach is
36. A Drinking and driving is
37. B Drinking and driving are
38. B theses were
39. B cheerleaders are
40. A one is
41. B The Who were
42. B chocolates are
43. B radii are
44. B parents root
45. A lack is
46. B fungi are
47. A ability is
48. A running is
49. A Gin and tonic is
50. A game is

Problems with Pronouns

Diagnostic Test

Choose the correct pronoun. If neither of the pronouns is satisfactory, choose neither.

1. The bully told me that I had an ugly nose (A. which B. that) annoyed me.

2. (A. Who B. Whom) are you planning to give the tiara to?

3. My father is a professional boxer and he promises to teach (A. it B. that) to me when I turn eighteen.

4. Everyone except John and (A. I B. me) will be there.

5. I scored higher on the test than (A. he B. him).

6. (A. We B. Us) truckers are used to driving through the night.

7. After I got a wart on my finger, I prayed to God to remove (A. it B. him).

8. Apple will issue (A. its B. their) annual report next month.

9. I didn't turn in my homework yesterday. (A. Which B. That) will lower my grade.

10. Every single one of the football players will try (A. his B. their) best.

Problems with Pronouns

He   She   They

A **pronoun** is a word used to replace one or more nouns. The noun that it replaces is called the pronoun's **antecedent**. It is important to understand pronouns, their uses, their types, and their cases.

I. Types of Pronouns

A. Personal Pronouns

Personal pronouns refer to the *1st person*, *2nd person*, or *3rd person*, *singular* or *plural*.

Personal pronouns can act as subjects or objects, and they take the following forms:

	Subjective		Objective	
	Singular	Plural	Singular	Plural
1st Person	I	we	me	us
2nd Person	you	you (all)	you	you (all)
3rd Person	he/she/it	they	him/she/it	them

Examples: *I* am kicking *him*. (*I* is the subject, *him* is the direct object.)

              She is buying *you* candy. (*She* is the subject, *you* is the indirect object.)

B. Possessive Pronouns

***Possessive* pronouns** answer the question: Whose? A possessive pronoun may act as a stand-alone substitute for a possessive noun (Mary's = *hers*), or as a possessive adjective modifying a noun (Mary's book = *her* book). Note that the form changes (from *her* to *hers*, from *my* to *mine*, from *our* to *ours*, etc.) depending on whether the possessive pronoun precedes and modifies another noun or stands alone.

<u>Singular</u>	<u>Plural</u>
my, mine	our, ours
your, yours (singular you)	your, yours ("you all")
his, her, hers, its	their, theirs

Examples: I like *her* book. (possessive pronoun precedes another noun)

The book is *hers*. (possessive pronoun stands alone)

I like *my* book. (possessive pronoun precedes another noun)

The book is *mine*. (possessive pronoun stands alone)

I like *your* book. (possessive pronoun precedes another noun)

The book is *yours*. (possessive pronoun stands alone)

C. Reflexive and Intensive Pronouns

Reflexive pronouns are used when the subject acts on itself.

Examples: I hurt *myself*.

She hurt *herself*.

He hurt *himself*.

Make *yourself* some lunch.

Intensive pronouns strengthen or emphasize the subject.

Examples: The boy *himself* saw the robber.

The girls went door-to-door *themselves*.

D. Interrogative Pronouns

An ***interrogative pronoun*** introduces a question that requires more than a yes or no answer. The interrogative pronouns are **who, which, whose, whom,** and **what**.

Examples: *What* are you doing tonight?

Whose chair is that?

Who are you?

Which is your favorite?

Whom do you trust?

What do you want?

E. Demonstrative Pronouns

Demonstrative pronouns answer the question "Which?" It specifies a particular person or thing. The demonstrative pronouns are:

	Singular	Plural
	this	**these**
	that	**those**

Examples: *This* is delicious!

Those do not belong to you.

F. Indefinite Pronouns

Indefinite pronouns refer imprecisely, or indefinitely, to people, places, things, or ideas. The antecedent is either unknown or simply unexpressed.

All	Either	Much	Somebody
Another	Everybody	Neither	Someone
Any	Everyone	Nobody	Something
Anybody	Everything	None	Whatever
Anyone	Few	No one	Whichever
Anything	Many	One	Whoever
Both	More	Several	Whomever
Each	Most	Some	

Examples: *Nobody* expected the teacher to throw a pop quiz.

Whoever hit that home run is very strong.

"Never was so *much* owed by so *many* to so *few*." –Winston Churchill

G. Relative Pronouns

Relative pronouns are pronouns that are used to begin subordinate clauses, especially adjective clauses. They tell, refer to, or are related to a word or idea that preceded them. The relative pronouns are **who, whom, whose, which, that,** and **what.**

Examples: The president presented a purple heart to the man *who lost his leg in Iraq.*

The man *whom you saw* is the town police chief.

My friend Jake, *whose car is parked in my parking spot*, offered to give me a ride home.

I don't know *which is more important*.

I want to report to your parents the dog *that ate your homework*!

The teacher told me *what to do*.

II. Case

Pronouns should be in the right case. The three cases in English are nominative, objective, and possessive.

A. Nominative Case for Subjects

The nominative case is used for the subject of a verb or for pronouns that follow a linking verb and stand for the subject. Nominative pronouns include *I, he, she, we, they, who,* and *whoever*.

- Sally is a cheerleader. - *Sally* is the subject of *is*
- She is a cheerleader. - *She* is the subject of *is*
- The cheerleader is she. - *she* follows the linking verb *is* and stands for the subject *the cheerleader*
- Joe is a bartender. - *Joe* is the subject of *is*
- He is a bartender. - *He* is the subject of *is*
- The bartender is he. - *he* follows the linking verb *is* and stands for the subject *the bartender*
- He is going to the mall. - *He* is the subject of *is going*
- I like people who tell jokes. - *who* is the subject of *tell jokes*
- I can throw the ball farther than he (can). - *he* is the subject of the implied verb *can*
- He can sing louder than I (can). - *I* is the subject of the implied verb *can*
- The woman is she. - *she* follows the linking verb *is* and stands for the subject *the woman*
- The players on the team are we. - *we* follows the linking verb *are* and stands for the subject *the players*
- Can I help you? - *I* is the subject of *can help*

I	Can help	you

B. Objective Case

The objective case is used for receivers of an action, for pronouns next to an infinitive, or for the object of a preposition. Objective pronouns include *me, him, her, us, them, whom,* and *whomever.*

- John gave the ball to <u>him.</u> - him receives the action of the verb "give"
- <u>Whom</u> do you love? - Whom receives the action of the verb "love"
- I know the waitress to be <u>her.</u> - her follows an infinitive
- I know <u>him</u> to be the man in charge. - him precedes an infinitive
- John requires his opponent to be <u>him.</u> - him follows an infinitive
- Everyone except <u>them</u> is going to be there. - them is the object of the preposition "except"
- No one on the team including John and <u>me</u> is allowed to drink alcohol. - me is the object of the preposition "including"
- Can we meet <u>her</u> now? - her receives the action of the verb "can meet"

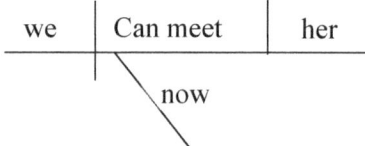

C. Possessive Case

Recall that possessive pronouns answer the question: whose? Both nouns and pronouns can be in the possessive case.

- The <u>alligator's</u> teeth are very sharp.
- The alligator showed me <u>its</u> teeth.
- The pink computer is <u>John's.</u>
- The blue computer is <u>hers.</u>

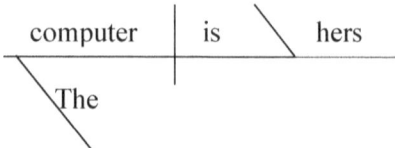

If there is a noun or pronoun before a gerund, then that noun or pronoun needs to be in the possessive case.

- <u>Jack's sweating</u> was easy to see. (sweating is a gerund)
- <u>His</u> swimming was faster than normal. (swimming is a gerund)

Be aware that a participle, an adjective that comes from a verb, can also end in *-ing*.

- I saw a boy sweating profusely. (sweating is a participle)
- The boy swimming in the water was very talented. (swimming is a participle)

Drill 1 *Choose the correct pronoun and explain why your answer is correct.*
1. (A. I B. Me C. My) walking gradually sped up until it became a jog.
2. After my brother started crying, I gave the remote to (A. he B. him C. his).
3. I can run much faster than (A. she B. her C. hers).
4. Between you and (A. I B. me C. my), I think that our teacher is really nice.
5. The pencil that is underneath the table is (A. I B. me C. my D. mine)
6. I like comedians (A. who B. whom) tell funny jokes.
7. (A. Who B. Whom) did you talk to yesterday?
8. The man in the mirror is (A. I B. me C. my)

III. Agreement in Number

The number of the pronoun must match the number of the antecedent. Refer to the section on Subject-Verb Agreement for advice on how to tell if a subject is singular or plural.

Singular pronouns include *he, she, you, me, this, that*, etc.

- Each person at the party threw his or her hat in the air.
- Either Sarah or Jane left her uniform at home.
- Every one of the football players tried his best.

Plural pronouns include *these, those, they, us, ours*, etc.
- These diseases are very contagious.
- Some of the citizens are not paying their taxes.
- All but Jake and us are planning to go to the beach today.

Never use *they, them, their,* or *themselves* for a singular antecedent.

Drill 2 *Choose the correct pronoun and explain why your answer is correct.*
1. Please retrieve (A. that B. those) die from the cabinet.
2. Half of the firefighters lost (A. his or her life B. their lives).
3. Every single one of the cheerleaders threw (A. her B. their) pom-pom in the air.
4. Nobody remembered to turn in (A. his B. their) homework assignment.
5. The policeman, who had many stamps, was scared that someone would steal (A. it B. them)
6. Each of the cakes would taste better with more chocolate in (A. its B. their) frosting.

IV. Agreement in Person

Don't use *one* and *you* in the same sentence to refer to the same person.

- Wrong: If <u>one</u> of you boys is hungry, then ~~you~~ should take a break and have some lunch. (Wrong since the one and you is the same person)
  Fixed: If <u>one</u> of you boys in hungry, then <u>he</u> should take a break and have some lunch.
- Whenever <u>you</u> are ready, <u>you</u> should let <u>me</u> know.
- If some<u>one</u> is willing to give <u>you</u> one million dollars, then <u>you</u> should take it. (Fine since the one and you are different people)

Don't use *it* to refer to a person and don't use *he, she, her,* etc., for things. (There are some exceptions, as with ships.)

Examples: The company sought to raise <u>its</u> profits.

The army lost <u>its</u> guns.

The army soldier lost <u>his</u> gun.

Old Ironside is a beautiful ship that makes Americans feel proud when they see <u>her</u>.

V. Ambiguous Reference

A.   One Clear Antecedent

Pronouns should never be ambiguous or vague. They need to have exactly one clear antecedent.

- Jack and John entered ~~his~~ room (should be Jack's room or John's room)
- There is a spot on the television. Can you see ~~it~~? (Corrected: Can you see the spot on the television?)

Drill 3 *Find and correct any errors in each sentence. Put "no errors" for grammatically correct sentences.*
1. The policeman, who recently arrested a gangster, is afraid that he is in danger.
2. Whenever you girls are ready to start, she should let me know.
3. You included a swear word in your essay. Can you delete it?
4. Some of the company's employees have talked to me about their experiences.
5. After animal rights activists released most of the zoo animals, they ran away.
6. Every deciduous tree sheds her leaves once per year.

B. Which and That Refer to Nouns

Which is used to introduce a clause that adds details to something, and *that* is used to introduce a clause that helps specify something.

- The man brought in a lunch bag, *which* looked as if it belonged to a third-grade girl. (*which looked as if it belonged to a third-grade girl* describes the lunch bag)
- Go sit at the chair *that* is next to the fireplace. (*that is next to the fireplace* helps specify the chair)

All pronouns, including *which* and *that,* need to refer to a specific noun, pronoun, or gerund. A pronoun can't refer to an adjective, adverb, phrase, or clause.

- Jack jumped on his bed, which annoyed his mother. (The preceding noun closest to which is bed. Did the bed annoy his mother? Corrected: Jack's jumping on his bed annoyed his mother.)
- There are snakes on the plane! That is dangerous! (The preceding noun closest to that is plane. Is the plane dangerous? Corrected: We are in danger because there are snakes on the plane.)
- She is constantly hungry, which causes her to spend a lot on groceries. (hungry is an adjective. Pronouns can't refer to adjectives. Corrected: Her constant hunger causes her to spend a lot on groceries.)

C. People are not Actions

Pronouns must mean the exact same thing as their antecedents. Actions (like surfing, running, fishing) are different from people who do the actions (like surfers, runners, or fishermen).

- I am surprised that my brother, a professional tennis player, never taught it to me. (should be tennis)
- After the man yodeled, I knew that he was a good one. (should be a yodeler)
- The boy wanted to become an actor, but he never pursued it. (should be an acting career)

Drill 4 *Find and correct any errors in each sentence. Put "no errors" for grammatically correct sentences.*
1. Albert Einstein developed the theory of relativity, a theory which was used to develop nuclear energy and GPS technology.
2. There are many fishermen in my family, but I am not good at it.
3. Engineering, which depends heavily on science, never came easily to me, but I decided to become one anyway.
4. I decided to run for mayor. That meant that I needed to convince people to vote for me.

5. The magician proceeded to walk on water, which impressed me so much that I decided to learn it.
6. Since she is a comedian, I assumed that she liked it.

VI. Pronoun Peculiarities

There are several important pronouns that sound the same but that differ in meaning.

A.   It's / Its

"It's" is an abbreviation for "it is."
- It's moving towards the house. (It is moving towards the house)

"Its" is a pronoun that assigns possession to a noun, subject, or thing.
- Something is making its way towards the house. ("Its" gives the "something" possession of way")

B.   Who's / Whose

"Who's" is an abbreviation for "who has" and "who is."
- Who's going to the baseball game? (Who is going to the baseball game?)
- Who's done the homework? (Who has done the homework?)

"Whose" is a pronoun that assigns possession to a person or thing.
- Whose phone is on the table? ("Whose" establishes that the phone belongs to someone)
- We should consider whose greed for money led us to this scandal. ("Whose" establishes that someone has a "greed for money")

C.   They're / Their / There

"They're" is an abbreviation for "they are."
- They're ready to go to the Johnsons' pool. (They are ready to go to the Johnson's pool.)

"Their" is a pronoun that assigns possession to more than one person(s) or thing(s).
- Companies must reevaluate their systems of organization when profits and revenues begin decreasing. ("their" establishes that "systems of organization" belongs to "companies")

"There" is an adverb that establishes a place, position, or thing. "There's" is an abbreviation for "there is."
- There is a place in California called Stinson Beach.
- There is a movie called *The Shawshank Redemption.*

- Stranded on this island, we are trying to get over there to the mainland.
- There's a bird in the trees.

D. Everyone / Every one

"Everyone" is a pronoun synonymous with "everybody," referring to all people in a group.
- The new update to the software will help everyone work more efficiently.

"Every one" refers to each individual member of a group. "Every one" is often followed by the preposition "of."
- The school principal personally congratulated every one of the students who graduated this year. ("every one" singles out each individual "student")

E. Who / Whom

"Who" is a pronoun used for referring to people who are subjects.
- He did not know who could be trusted. (subject pronoun)

"Whom" is a pronoun used for referring to people who are objects.
- He did not know whom he trusted. (object pronoun)

F. Myself

"Myself" is a reflexive pronoun that reflects on something you did to yourself or for yourself. It is not a substitute for "I" or for "me." "Myself" can only be used if "I" or "me" was used previously in the sentence.
- Incorrect: My best friend and myself are going to the beach.
- Correct: I injured myself.

Pronoun Exercises

Choose the correct pronoun. If neither of the pronouns is satisfactory, choose neither.

1. (A. Who B. Whom) are you planning to take to prom?
2. If someone gives you a present, you should thank (A. they B. them).
3. I think that Google is a great corporation. That is why I want to work for (A. it B. them).
4. Everyone except for Jake and (A. I B. me) is going to the concert.
5. Were you as tired as (A. I B. me) last night?
6. The man whom I talked to is (A. he B. him).
7. (A. This B. These) crises happen all of the time.
8. In the movie *Reservoir Dogs*, a robber cuts off the ears of a police officer, (A. which B. that) causes him to bleed.
9. I met a skater and he convinced me to try (A. it B. that).
10. The student poured paint all over the teacher's car. (A. That B. Which) caused the teacher to scream in agony.
11. Jack brought (A. that B. those) dice to the meeting.
12. Nobody should expect (A. themself B. themselves) to get a perfect score on the test.
13. I know the man in black to be (A. he B. him).
14. My teacher sometimes expects too much from my brother and (A. I B. me).
15. The game was forfeited because of (A. James B. James') breaking of the rules.
16. Karen and (A. she B. her) decided to watch a movie.
17. The robber told the man to open (A. his B. its) wallet.
18. The boy liked Yale more than Princeton, (A. which B. that) irritated his parents because they wanted him to go to Princeton.
19. The man (A. who B. whom) I was chasing jumped off of the bridge.
20. Each one of you students is expected to turn in (A. your B. its) homework.
21. The rising temperature, (A. which B. that) made me want to stay inside, was over 90 degrees Fahrenheit.
22. I was surprised by (A. Jack B. Jack's) stealing.
23. After you finish your report on the movie, send (A. it B. them) to me.
24. (A. We B. Us) girls made you a cake.
25. I would marry no one other than (A. she B. her).

Pronoun Exercises

Choose the correct pronoun. If neither of the pronouns is satisfactory, choose neither.

26. Give the prize to (A. whoever B. whomever) finishes first.
27. She lacked money and health insurance, (A. which B. that) made it impossible to afford the surgery, so she decided to seek alternative treatments.
28. The man who I plan to attack is (A. he B. him).
29. I like baseball more than (A. her B. she).
30. The teacher hates (A. my B. me) speaking without raising my hand.
31. Among (A. we B. us) twelve truckers, Peter has driven the most highway miles.
32. After seeing a sword, I reached for (A. its B. it's) handle.
33. Just between you and (A. I B. me), I don't like chocolate.
34. After Halloween, every one of you boys is expected to donate (A. his B. your) candy to charity.
35. I like seeing Shirley and (A. he B. him) at the ice cream parlor on Friday nights.
36. I saw a woman dressed as a witch talking to a girl dressed as a ghost. (A. She B. It) looked spooky.
37. I am a great baseball player, but my brother hates (A. it B. that).
38. When the dog saw Jill, (A. it B. she) started jumping up and down.
39. Between you and (A. I B. me), that clock is off by five minutes.
40. The boys are (A. we B. us).
41. Her constant determination to do well in everything that she does, (A. which B. that) caused her to be admitted to Harvard, is enviable.
42. The Lincoln administration is well renowned for (A. his B. its) role in ending slavery in the United States.
43. Every one of the boys forgot to bring (A. his B. their) baseball glove.
44. If you make an accidental mark on your paper, you can use Wite-Out to remove (A. it B. them).
45. He is very strong, (A. which B. that) helps him throw the javelin very far.
46. The robot and (A. we B. us) were able to safely travel home.
47. Every member of the tennis team tried to win as many points as (A. she B. they) could.
48. The baseball player hit the ball over the fence, (A. that B. which) caused the home team to win the game.
49. Every single one of the cheerleaders respects (A. herself B. themselves).
50. Hoping to arrive early to the theatre, I was dismayed by my (A. father B. father's) taking so long to dress.

Answers

Diagnostic

1. Neither - both pronouns make it seem like the nose instead of the remark annoyed him
2. B. Whom
3. Neither -should be boxing
4. B. me
5. A. he (did)
6. A. We - subject
7. Neither - should be the wart
8. A. its
9. Neither - don't use a pronoun to refer to an entire sentence
10. A. his

Drill 1

1. C. My - pronoun before a gerund
2. B. him - receiver of verb
3. A. she - subject of implied verb can
4. B. me - object of preposition "between"
5. D. mine (assuming that the author of the sentence isn't a pencil)
6. A. who - subject of verb tell
7. B. Whom - receiver of verb
8. A. I - follows linking verb and stands for subject

Drill 2

1. A. that - die is singular
2. B. their lives - Half of the firefighters is plural
3. A. her - Every single one makes the subject singular
4. A. his - nobody is singular
5. B. them - stamps are plural
6. B. its - each of the cakes is singular

Drill 3

1. He is ambiguous - The policeman, who recently arrested a gangster, is afraid that the gangster is in danger OR The policeman is afraid that he is in danger, because he recently arrested a gangster
2. Mixed you and she - Whenever you girls are ready to start, you should let me know. (or one of you should let me know)
3. It is ambiguous - Can you delete the swear word in your essay?
4. No errors
5. They is ambiguous - After animal rights activists released most of the zoo animals, the animals ran away OR After animal rights activists released most of the zoo animals, the activists ran away
6. Trees are gender neutral in prose - Every deciduous tree sheds its leaves once per year.

Drill 4

1. no errors
2. it doesn't have a valid antecedent - There are many fishermen in my family, but I am not good at fishing.
3. one doesn't have a valid antecedent - Engineering, which depends heavily on science, never came easily to me, but I decided to become an engineer anyway.
4. That doesn't have a valid antecedent - Because I decided to run for mayor, I needed to convince people to vote for me.
5. which and it don't have valid antecedents - The magician's walk on water impressed me so much that I decided to learn magic (or the trick).
6. it doesn't have a valid antecedent - Since she is a comedian, I assumed that she liked comedy (or her job).

Exercises

1. B Whom
2. Neither (You should thank him or her)
3. A it
4. B me
5. A I (implied was)
6. A he
7. B These
8. Neither (The police officer doesn't cause himself to bleed. The cutting causes him to bleed. Corrected: In the movie *Reservoir Dogs*, a robber cuts off the ears of a police officer, who then begins to bleed.)
9. Neither (should be try skating)
10. Neither (both lack a viable antecedent)
11. B those
12. Neither (should be himself or herself)
13. B him
14. B me
15. B James'
16. A she
17. Neither (ambiguous)
18. Neither (Princeton doesn't irritate his parents. The boy's preference irritates his parents.)
19. B whom
20. Neither (don't mix one and you)
21. A. which
22. B Jack's
23. Neither (ambiguous)
24. A We
25. B her
26. A whoever
27. Neither (Does health insurance make it impossible to afford surgery?)
28. A he
29. B she
30. A my
31. B us
32. A its
33. B me
34. A his
35. B him
36. Neither (ambiguous)
37. Neither (should be baseball)
38. A it (*she* is fine for a dog, but not if the sentence would be ambiguous)
39. B me

40. A we
41. Neither (don't use *which* to refer to a phrase)
42. B its
43. A his
44. Neither (ambiguous)
45. Neither (*which* shouldn't refer to an adjective)
46. A we
47. A she (*they* is definitely incorrect, but *she* can be correct for a female team)
48. Neither (did the fence cause the home team to win?)
49. A herself
50. B father's

Sentence Fragments

Diagnostic Test

For each exercise, identify all the sentence fragments.

1. I have many hobbies. Swimming, playing tennis, and painting pictures of dogs. What are your favorite hobbies?

2. I never knew where the man liked to play tennis. Or even when he liked to play. I don't think I will ever know.

3. To open the pickle jar. I had to use tape to get a good grip. It worked.

4. I decided to tell her my biggest secret. That I stole thousands of dollars from my cousin, Ethan. What a secret!

5. While I was waiting for the train. I saw a man pickpocket my friend, Samuel. Immediately afterwards, I chased after the thief.

6. I could smell marijuana in my daughter's breath. Therefore, while I sat in my chair and listened to her story. I knew that she wasn't telling the truth.

7. Swimming in the ocean. The deep sea diver felt right at home. He loved feeling the cold water and seeing the life that lived within it.

8. Bang! I didn't feel anything, but then I looked down at my left leg. It was covered in blood.

9. Last night, I forgot to lock my apartment door. When I woke up, I saw that the door was ajar and that my laptop was missing. If only I had remembered to lock the door.

10. It came. I stared into the monster's dark black eyes. I knew that it wouldn't stop following me until I was dead.

Sentence Fragments

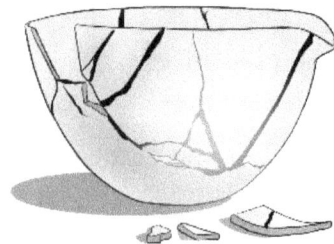

A sentence is a group of words with a subject and a verb which together make a complete thought.

Examples: ***Jack*** ran.

Jay likes Ann-Marie.

Jack	ran	
Jay	likes	Ann-Marie

The following examples below lack the combination of a subject and a verb that together make a complete thought.

Examples: Going to the market.
(***Fragment***: It has no subject)

Todd needed.
(***Fragment***: *needed*, which is a transitive verb, has no direct object)

After running for hours.
(***Fragment***: Incomplete thought)

When I went to the store.
(***Fragment***: Incomplete thought)

Because I was exhausted.
(***Fragment***: Incomplete thought)

Each fraction of a complete thought is a ***fragment***. While sentence fragments may be used occasionally for literary effect, they have no place in formal writing because they do not contribute to clarity of meaning.

I. Independent and Dependent Clauses

A *clause* is a group of related words containing a subject and a verb.

If a clause makes sense on its own, it is known as an ***independent clause***. If the independent clause is part of a sentence with a subordinate clause, the independent clause is called the ***main clause***.

Examples: Tom is a rather large man.

   The square root of four is two.

   Jason loves eating broccoli.

A ***dependent*** or ***subordinate*** clause contains a subject and a verb combination but cannot stand on its own. A dependent clause needs the rest of the sentence to make sense. Therefore, a dependent clause alone is a sentence fragment. Recall that there are three types of dependent clauses: adjectival (modify nouns and pronouns), adverbial (modify verbs, adjectives, and adverbs), and noun (functions as a noun).

Examples: *While I was preparing for work*, I packed my computer. (adverbial clause)

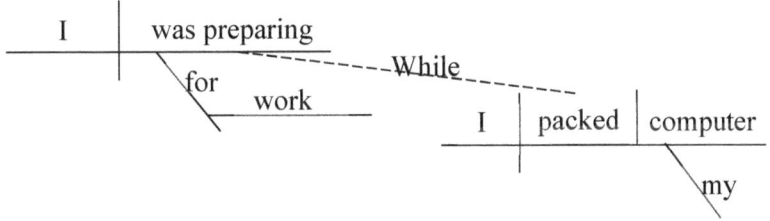

   I saw the tall man *who bumped his head.* (adjectival clause)

   James asked *where he should go.* (noun clause)

Any of the previous ***dependent clauses*** on their own would be a ***sentence fragment***.

Examples: *While I was preparing for work.* (fragment)

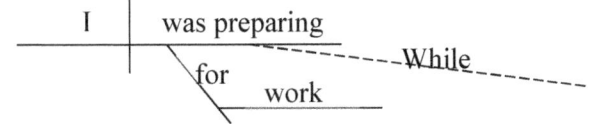

   Who bumped his head. (fragment)

   Where he should go. (fragment)

Drill 1 *Underline independent clauses once and dependent clauses twice.*
1. When you finish reading that book, you should try reading this one.
2. I don't know how warm it is outside.
3. The man who wrote the book died before it was published.
4. Please put away your dishes after you wash them.
5. Walking to the store, the young boy tripped when he stubbed his toe.
6. The hospital where I was born was recently bought by a local millionaire.

* Note that verbal phrases (gerund such as *on entering the gallery*, participial such as *running through the maze*, infinitive such as *to learn French*) are not clauses, because they do not have a subject and a verb.

Examples: After running for hours, the girl finally took a water break. - *After running for hours* is a gerund phrase, and so *the girl finally took a water break* is the only clause in the sentence.

                Thinking about his dog, the boy decided to go home. - *Thinking about his dog* is a participial phrase, and so *the boy decided to go home* is the only clause in this sentence.

Sentence Fragments Exercises

For each exercise, identify all of the sentence fragments.

1. Paul Pierce has a special place in my heart. I always wanted to meet him. Having been, as a young boy, a devoted fan of the Boston Celtics.

2. Neil Armstrong is the first man to step on the moon. Neil stepped. He subsequently became a legend.

3. General Motors began building automobiles early in the 20th century. The forerunner of several improved car engines developed by the staff there. The staff helped make the automobile industry what it is today.

4. Police officers in Lawrence, Kansas are reported by the federal government to have confiscated several pounds of cocaine from a high-profile drug dealer. While he was attempting to sell the cocaine to an undercover cop. The drug dealer could face up to twenty years in prison.

5. My boss surprised everyone in the office with thousand-dollar bonuses. Which I plan to use to help pay off my student loans. I currently owe over $50,000.

6. I came. I saw. I conquered.

7. Food was what I needed. No one could tell me where to find the nearest restaurant. Or even where I could go to find a snack.

8. Yesterday, I bought a new watch. Because my old watch stopped running after I wore it in the pool. I even tried putting it in rice to dry it out.

9. While my parents talked to me about different colleges. I thought about what I wanted to eat for breakfast. I decided to eat Frosted Flakes, which is a type of cereal.

10. To be or not to be. That is the question. Whether 'tis nobler in the mind to suffer the slings and arrows of outrageous fortune, or to take arms against a sea of troubles, and by opposing end them?

Answers

Diagnostic

1. Swimming, playing tennis, and painting pictures of dogs.

2. Or even when he liked to play.

3. To open the pickle jar.

4. That I stole thousands of dollars from my cousin, Ethan. What a secret!

5. While I was waiting for the train

6. Therefore, while I sat in my chair and listened to her story.

7. Swimming in the ocean.

8. Bang! (it is a fragment, but it is fine to include fragments in literature)

9. If only I had remembered to lock the door.

10. No sentence fragments

Drill 1

1. <u>When you finish reading the book</u>, <u>you should try reading this one</u>.

2. <u>I don't know</u> <u>how warm it is outside</u>.

3. <u>The man</u> <u>who wrote the book</u> <u>died before it was published</u>.

4. <u>Please put away your dishes</u> <u>after you wash them</u>.

5. <u>Walking to the store, the young boy tripped</u> <u>when he stubbed his toe</u>.

6. <u>The hospital</u> <u>where I was born</u> <u>was recently bought by a local millionaire</u>.

Exercises

1. Having been, as a young boy, a devoted fan of the Boston Celtics.

2. No sentence fragments

3. The forerunner of several improved car engines developed by the staff there.

4. While he was attempting to sell the cocaine to an undercover cop.

5. Which I plan to use to help pay off my student loans.

6. No sentence fragments

7. Or even where I could go to find a snack.

8. Because my old watch stopped running after I wore it in the pool.

9. While my parents talked to me about different colleges.

10. To be or not to be. Whether 'tis nobler in the mind to suffer the slings and arrows of outrageous fortune, or to take arms against a sea of troubles, and by opposing end them?

First Cumulative Review

For each sentence, determine whether it is grammatically correct. If it is grammatically incorrect, identify the type of error:

Verb - V   Subject Verb Agreement - A   Pronoun - P   Fragment - F

(V, A, P, F)

1. After the damages to your car from the crash were assessed, your insurance pays the bills.

2. If only I could tell the difference between an alligator and a crocodile.

3. If two years ago the College Boards had not modified the SAT to make it more to the liking of juniors and seniors in high school, then more students will have signed up for the ACT, which more and more students found easier to take.

4. Between you and me, I heard John say, "My brother tried to sell me illicit substances, but I wouldn't buy any of them."

5. The promotion I received last week was long overdue; I worked for this company for fifteen years.

6. Every one of the doctors who have prescribed our medication raves about its benefits.

7. Whether to help my brother pay off his student loans or save money for retirement.

8. To become a great swimmer, I decided to just go ahead and try it.

9. Walking through the jungle, I saw a snake that nearly frightened me to death.

10. My family came to this retreat every year for ten years.

11. After a great performance from Robert de Niro in *Taxi Driver*, the actor who later made a name for himself in classic movies such as *The Heat*, *The Godfather*, and *Goodfellas*.

12. Each of the students is responsible for bringing in their own lunch.

13. Us baseball players need to stick together, even when other people try to pull us apart.

14. The policeman, along with his two daughters, are visiting the place where his wife was murdered.

15. I was surprised that not one of my children, whom I love dearly, are planning to attend my brother's funeral.

16. Approaching the finish line, I felt like one of those runners who races professionally.

17. We lived in this city for five years before my mother decided to have us relocate to an affluent suburb.

18. As a part of the staging process to make the home ready to be put up for sale to the public, the interior decorator recommended that the homeowner move the family portrait to a more suitable spot above the fireplace rather than keep it in its regular but incongruous spot to the left of the bassinet.

19. Once I realize what I want to do when I grow up, so I can better prepare for my future.

20. Unfortunately, my favorite guitar is one of those instruments that costs more than I can afford.

21. At least one of my brothers is planning to tell the police that he saw me holding a gun last night.

22. Going down a big drop, the rollercoaster accelerated, which frightened me.

23. When the cheerleaders were getting dressed at the same time when a reporter was secretly observing them, they were not aware of it.

24. I am so lucky that the woman whom I married is a kind and loving person.

25. Watching *Titanic* seven times, the impressionable teenage girl tells all her friends what happens to Leonardo DiCaprio and his romantic partner Kate Winslet.

26. I asked someone to give me their pencil—but no one answered me.

27. According to the student handbook, nobody is allowed to dress in clothing that shows their torso.

28. There is no reason for the pundit to continue his argument now that the facts on which it was based had been discredited.

29. Despite trying my best and understanding what was asked of me. I did not pass the test.

30. The other day I met the owner of the new gourmet restaurant in town, a man who has been imprisoned by the Nazis during World War II, though for what reason he did not disclose.

31. The media were completely astonished. When the supposedly unhinged candidate won the election easily. His numbers had not been favorable in the pre-election polls.

32. The girl looked around the corner and froze. The horrifying, grotesque apparition stood right there. Its chilling stare seemed to pierce her consciousness.

33. Andy Dufresne had a clear and moral purpose. To escape the binds of the corrupted system that had wrongly imprisoned him long ago for a crime that he had not committed.

34. In the graveyard scene when Hamlet arrives and talks to the gravedigger, he encountered the grieving Laertes, whose sister had committed suicide.

35. Nobody except for you and me were smart enough to get a perfect score on the test, which covered multiplying and dividing fractions.

36. My brother is a professional tennis player, but I don't even know how to play it.

37. Inside the walls live a ghost that makes spooky noises during the night.

38. Dantes pushed aside the light metal sheet to reveal the treasure. About thirty chests, filled to the brim with gold, silver, diamonds, and jewels.

39. Neither my closest friends nor my wife are going to attend my last baseball game of the season, which started in June.

40. Not one of the students who are on my hockey team plan to bring her skates to school.

41. To improve your mastery of vocabulary, one should review words that are elusive.

42. To prepare for the SAT, everybody in my class studied for at least an hour at his or her home.

43. After waiting for hours, I caught a frog by using my giant bucket, but I decided to let it go.

44. The percentage of students who know multiple programming languages are rising.

45. The Secretary of Defense states that the American soldiers in Afghanistan will struggle against the Taliban until the Americans conquered and destroyed all of the Taliban strongholds.

46. Alexandre Dumas developed an affinity for Napoleon Bonaparte's principles of social equality and classical liberalism. Even though Alexandre's father, a general of the French army, had a falling out with Emperor Napoleon.

47. To better prepare myself for school, I almost went to a tutoring agency.

48. Not one of the cheerleaders is happy, which makes me very sad.

49. Approaching the finish line, I felt like one of those runners who races professionally.

50. My charisma along with my humility make me a wonderful boyfriend.

51. My younger brother always seems to be happy, which makes him fun to be around.

52. Out of breath and completely distraught, the man begged the Mafia boss to return his wife. The boss refused. Any precedent of mercy would diminish the gang's notoriety.

53. The teacher of Spanish opened her drawer in which she kept her tests and then hands out one of her favorite exams.

54. There is a lot of restaurants that offer delivery, but most of them charge extra for the service.

55. Whether employees at the department or their boss are issuing this license is none of my concern.

56. In an age when often the public hears in the news about football players behaving badly, the public has come to believe that any football coach who does not set a high standard for their player, is letting down both the parents and the team.

57. Some credit cards are structured for certain consumer activities. Such as frequent flyer miles, which benefit the consumers so much that they work relentlessly to acquire the points necessary to redeem the cards' promised rewards.

58. The government is about to enter its second shutdown in the past three months. Because both political parties are holding back from serious negotiations to end the impasse.

59. The teacher told the student that he needed to review his files because the next assignment would follow from the previous one and would show continuity in the sequential relationship of each essay topic.

60. If I would have helped you with your studying, we could have prevented you from failing the test.

61. In the national public speaking contest for middle school students, it was particularly important during the impromptu round that each speaker come up with their own imaginative and spontaneous presentation without any time beforehand to either prepare or rehearse.

62. The bar is full of drunk and obnoxious characters. Especially on late weekend nights when college students after their football game, regardless of victory or defeat, come in for hours of celebration that lead to their inebriation.

63. In the national public speaking contest for middle school students, it was particularly important during the impromptu round that each speaker come up with their own imaginative and spontaneous presentation without any time beforehand to either prepare or rehearse.

64. After she had left the bar, and began walking alone back to her apartment, she noticed that though the streets were well lit, they were so deserted that she saw so hardly no one out except some street sweepers who worked for the city.

65. Inspiring viewers and bringing into question the very nature of man, *Citizen Kane* is one of those legendary movies that has survived the test of time.

66. None of the loss to his net worth and damage to his reputation wouldn't have occurred if the businessmen had only avoided driving under the influence, a dangerous decision that resulted in the loss of life.

67. Of all the types of law available, corporate law was what the student chose. An area requiring excellent communication, analytical, writing, and argumentative skills that a diligent student will need in the future as he enters the competitive business world.

68. In the huddle before the game just after the coach exhorted his team to resist with all their might the offense of the opposing team, and reminding them that it is the hungry wolf that fights, he demanded that each player shows their commitment to the fight by shouting one after the other, "Yes sir."

69. Every one of the cars located in the parking spaces behind the building have a Massachusetts license plate.

70. Experience and professional merit is integral to securing higher level internships.

71. If I were she, I would consider majoring in accounting, a subject closely associated with math; after all, she excels in her advanced placement calculus and statistics classes.

72. Desperately hoping to augment his salary and to push his own racial and political agenda. The actor orchestrated a hoax in which he made it appear that he was the victim of a physical assault that was a hate crime. It is disgusting to see wealthy celebrities pushing false narratives in such a fashion.

73. To many Americans, Harvard is considered to be not only a superior university, but also a very old and venerable one, even though in England, France, Spain, and Italy, scholars have founded superior universities centuries earlier than Harvard.

74. The Council of Trent started reforming the Catholic Church because many of the domains of Europe would be falling to Protestantism.

75. Robert can surf the strong waves at the beach better than you or I. Even when there is a hurricane.

76. By the time today's kindergarteners graduate from high school, educational curricula have changed drastically.

77. Are my black sweatshirt and gray sweatpants there in the locker?

78. Despite opposition from environmental groups, the CEO refused to promise that he wouldn't move forward with a new plant.

79. Although highway speed limits aren't completely necessary, as demonstrated by the autobahn in Germany, they have another purpose. To financially support police

departments via speeding tickets, which is a source of revenue that is integral to the maintenance of the officers and payrolls.

80. Hoping to secure recognition and reap the full financial rewards of the film industry. The Lumiere Brothers worked tirelessly in France to develop film technologies that were superior to those of their competitor, Thomas Edison.

First Cumulative Review Answers

Answers may vary.

1. V - damages from the crash have been assessed

2. F - dependent clause

3. V - students would have signed up

4. Correct

5. V - I have worked for this company for fifteen years

6. Correct

7. F - incomplete thought

8. P - Ambiguous reference: "it" lacks a clear antecedent

9. Correct

10. V - My family has come to this retreat

11. F - incomplete thought

12. P - his or her own lunch

13. P - we baseball players

14. A - policeman... is visiting

15. A - one of my children... is planning

16. A - runners who race

17. V - we had lived

18. Correct

19. F - incomplete thought

20. A - instruments that cost more

21. Correct

22. P - Ambiguous reference: "which" lacks a clear antecedent

23. P - Ambiguous reference: "it" lacks a clear antecedent

24. Correct

25. V - Having watched

26. P - his or her pencil

27. P - his or her torso

28. V - have been discredited

29. F - incomplete thought

30. V - who had been

31. F - second cluster of words is an incomplete thought

32. Correct

33. F - second cluster of words is an incomplete thought

34. V - he encounters

35. A - was not were

36. P - Ambiguous reference: "it" lacks a clear antecedent

37. A - lives a ghost

38. F - second cluster of words is an incomplete thought

39. A - nor my wife is going

40. A - one of the students... plans to bring her skates to school

41. P - switches between one and you

42. Correct

43. P - Ambiguous reference: "it" lacks a clear antecedent

44. A - percentage is rising

45. V - until the Americans conquer and destroy

46. F - second cluster of words is an incomplete thought

47. Correct

48. P - Ambiguous reference: "which" lacks a clear antecedent

49. A - runners who race professionally

50. A - charisma… makes me a wonderful boyfriend

51. P - Ambiguous reference: "which" lacks a clear antecedent

52. Correct

53. V - and then handed out

54. A - there are… restaurants

55. A - boss is issuing

56. P - for his player

57. F - the second cluster of words is an incomplete thought

58. F - the second cluster of words is an incomplete thought

59. P - the student needed to check the student's files

60. V - If I had helped you

61. P - not their but his own

62. F - the second cluster of words is an incomplete thought

63. P - not their but his or her own

64. V - hardly anyone

65. A - movies that have

66. V - would have occurred

67. F - the second cluster of words is a dependent clause

68. *P - each player show his commitment*

69. *A - every one of... has a Massachusetts license plate*

70. *A - experience and professional merit are integral to*

71. *Correct*

72. *F - the first cluster of words is an incomplete thought*

73. *V - scholars founded superior universities*

74. *V - were falling to Protestantism*

75. *F - the second cluster of words is an incomplete thought*

76. *V - educational curricula will have changed*

77. *Correct*

78. *Correct*

79. *F - the second cluster of words is an incomplete thought*

80. *F - the first cluster of words is an incomplete thought*

SYNTAX

The order in which words appear in a sentence—adjectives, adverbs, nouns, pronouns, verbs, phrases, and clauses—is placed to convey the thought of the writer in a clear and logical way.

Misplaced Modifiers

Diagnostic Test

Below, indicate if the sentence is correct or in error. Make corrections to fix the sentence.

1. To win in tennis, your forehand is a crucial weapon.

2. Do you see the snail at the bottom of the fish tank that is eating a tiny piece of food?

3. After waiting in line for an hour, the rollercoaster ride was frightening yet exhilarating.

4. Lecturing on the history of ancient Greece, we learned from the speaker about Plato and Socrates.

5. The boy showed his parents his math test with great pride, which he got a perfect score on.

6. Turning the pages, I found many advertisements for sports apparel in this sporting magazine.

7. While still new, I donated my car to charity.

8. To get good grades, one must study for tests with confidence.

9. After running for hours, I told my assistant loudly to get me some ice-cold water.

10. Superman, who is a superhero, is so strong that he can easily defeat a tiger with his bare hands.

Misplaced Modifiers

The Mad Hatter will be serving tea to Alice in a cup.

Consider in the example below, what happens when we move the modifier *only*.

Example: Only I saw John. (Only modifies I. No one else saw John)

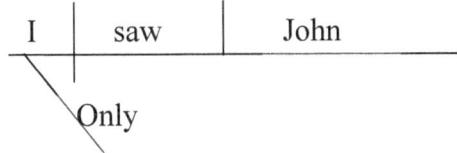

I only saw John. (Only modifies saw. I didn't do anything else with or to John)

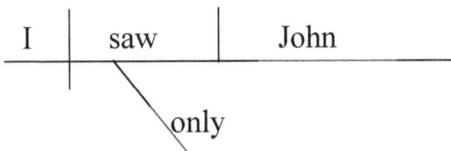

I saw only John. (Only modifies John. I didn't see anyone else)

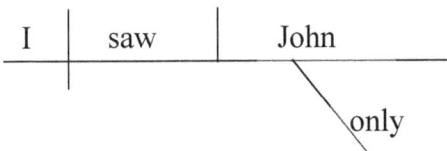

Modifiers should be near what they describe. Otherwise, the modifiers will describe something else. ***Misplaced modifiers*** can be in the form of adjectives, adverbs, phrases, or clauses. Recall that a phrase is a group of connected words that does not contain both a subject and a verb and a clause is a group of words containing the combination of a subject and a verb.

Consider what happens when we move the following modifiers.

Examples: I gave lemonade to the children in plastic cups. (*In plastic cups* is next to *children*, and so the sentence incorrectly implies that the children are in plastic cups)

I gave the children lemonade in plastic cups. (*In plastic cups* is next to *lemonade*, so the sentence correctly states that the lemonade is in plastic cups)

John saw an advertisement for a job in the parking lot. (*In the parking lot* is next to *job*, and so the sentence incorrectly implies that the job is in the parking lot)

John saw an advertisement in the parking lot for a job. (*In the parking lot* is next to *advertisement*, so the sentence correctly states that the advertisement is in the parking lot)

The waitress served a steak to the customer that was heavily salted. (*That was heavily salted* is next to *customer*, and so the sentence incorrectly implies that the customer is heavily salted)

The waitress served a steak that was heavily salted to the customer. (*That was heavily salted* is next to *steak*, so the sentence correctly states that the steak is heavily salted)

Drill 1 *Identify any modifier that might be misplaced and explain why it might be misplaced.*
1. He bought a dog for his brother called Fluffy.
2. I nearly ate all of the cookies in the cookie jar.
3. John threw the shirt in the trash that was ripped.
4. The captain saw a whale sitting in his chair.
5. We serve customers in our uniforms.
6. My assistant said on Friday he would finish revising the terms of the contract.
7. I went into the restaurant jumping up and down.
8. The professional fisherman placed a six-foot-long fish on the dock that he had just caught.

I. Dangling Elements

Whenever a sentence starts with a verbal phrase or phrase containing a verbal, the subject that the phrase refers to must immediately follow. Otherwise, the verbal phrase becomes a type of misplaced modifier called a ***dangling element***.

Examples: Wrong: ~~Swimming in the pool, my driver's license was lost.~~
Right: Swimming in the pool, I lost my driver's license.

Wrong: ~~To learn to drive, this manual is very useful.~~
Right: To learn to drive, one should read this manual.

Wrong: ~~Upon entering the school, my homework was dropped.~~
Right: Upon entering the school, I dropped my homework.

135

Refer to the Structure chapter on verbals for more information on participles, gerunds, and infinitives.

Drill 2 *Correct the sentences (without changing the opening phrases) and, as a bonus, identify the type of verbal used (infinitive, gerund, or participle). Each sentence has multiple possible corrections.*
1. Riding a unicycle, the students were amazed by the clown.
2. To sing the national anthem, the lyrics should be memorized beforehand.
3. On entering the theater, the seats were all taken.
4. To catch a leprechaun, a leprechaun must be correctly identified.
5. After running for hours, the ground started to look blurry.
6. Standing on the chair, the jar was now in reach.

II. Elliptical Clauses

An ***elliptical clause*** is a clause that is missing some words.

Examples: (Clause) I can throw the javelin farther than *he can*.
(Elliptical clause/gerund phrase) I can throw the javelin farther than *he*.

(Clause) He is stronger *than I am*.
(Elliptical clause) He is stronger *than I*.

Some dangling modifiers are elliptical clauses. This type of dangling element can be fixed by adding its subject into the clause or by having the subject immediately follow the clause.

Examples: Wrong: ~~When just a toddler, my parents took me to Disneyland.~~
Right: When I was just a toddler, my parents took me to Disneyland.
Right: When just a toddler, I was taken to Disneyland by my parents.

Wrong: ~~While blindfolded, my other senses were magnified.~~
Right: While I was blindfolded, my other senses were magnified.
Right: While blindfolded, I noticed my other senses getting stronger.

Drill 3 *Correct the sentence by editing the elliptical clause. There are multiple possible answers for each question.*
1. When only three years old, my mother was arrested.
2. If locked out of a car, Triple A can assist you.
3. While taking a shower, the fire alarm went off.
4. Though locked in a cage, the man was still afraid of the lion.
5. While sitting on a porch, the neighborhood seemed very calm.
6. If too difficult, you can retake the test another time.

Misplaced Modifier Exercises

Identify any modifiers that might be misplaced (including dangling elements) and why they might be misplaced. Make corrections to fix the sentence. Put N/A if no modifiers are misplaced.

1. Soggy with milk, he ate the delicious cookies.
2. To perform tests on animals, the animals should be treated humanely.
3. After receiving some complaints from cast members, we rehearsed for the play without our costumes.
4. I saw on television that the United States recently bombed ISIS in my bedroom.
5. Not understanding nearly all of the tested material, the student correctly answered only thirty percent of the multiple-choice questions.
6. The criminal got away with nearly stealing my brand-new car, but she was arrested last night.
7. To make peanut butter and jelly, the first step is to put two pieces of bread on your plate.
8. Despite receiving some complaints, the man kept a tiger in a large cage on his front lawn.
9. While designing a new website, an idea popped into my head.
10. Jumping up and down, I banged my head into the ceiling which hurt badly.
11. Kicking and screaming, the mom dragged her hysterical son out of the grocery store.
12. Since I only arrived in Las Vegas late last night, I have not had time to see the surrounding area.
13. In the fish tank, I dropped some food for my fish.
14. John wore a collared shirt to the job interview, which was unfortunately stained with ketchup.
15. After the birthday boy opened his other presents, I gave him a Star Wars action figure.
16. Walking for miles, my calves started to feel like they were grounded to a pulp.
17. My best friend, Jake, only arrived to pick me up after I frantically called his mother and told her to remind Jake that I needed a ride.
18. I learned that Luke Skywalker destroyed the Death Star by overhearing my friends' conversation.
19. To lift weights at our gym, the weights need to be cleaned after each use.
20. To save money, the family decided to serve all of their food to each other on reusable plates.

Answers

Diagnostic

1. Error - *to win in tennis* is a dangling element because your forehand can't win a tennis match. Corrected: A forehand is a crucial weapon used to win a tennis match.

2. Error - the clause *that was eating a tiny piece of food* needs to be next to the snail and not the fish tank. Corrected: Do you see the snail that is eating a tiny piece of food at the bottom of the fish tank?

3. Error - *after waiting in line for an hour* is a dangling element because the person and not the rollercoaster waited in line. Corrected: After waiting in line for an hour, I found the rollercoaster ride to be frightening yet exhilarating.

4. Error - *lecturing on the history of ancient Greece* is a dangling element because the speaker is more likely to be the person lecturing. Corrected: Lecturing on the history of ancient Greece, the speaker taught us about Plato and Socrates.

5. Error - the clause *which he got a perfect score on* needs to be next to the math test and not pride. Corrected: The boy proudly showed his parents his math test, which he got a perfect score on.

6. Error - *in this sporting magazine* is misplaced because it doesn't make sense for sports apparel to be inside of a magazine. Corrected: Turning the pages, I found many sports apparel advertisements in this sporting magazine.

7. Error - The prepositional phrase *while still new* is misplaced because it is the car that is new. Corrected: I donated my new car to charity.

8. Error - *with confidence* incorrectly implies that the tests are confident. Corrected: To get good grades, one must confidently study for tests.

9. Error - *loudly* is misplaced because it doesn't make sense for the assistant to need to be loud. Corrected: After running for hours, I loudly told my assistant to get me some ice-cold water.

10. Error - *with his bare hands* is misplaced because it doesn't make sense for the tiger to have Superman's hands. Corrected: Superman, who is a superhero, is so strong that he can easily and bare-handedly defeat a tiger

Drill 1

1. called Fluffy - means the brother is called Fluffy
2. nearly - means I came very close to eating every cookie
3. that was ripped - means the dumpster is ripped
4. sitting in his chair - means the whale is sitting in the chair
5. in our uniforms - means the customers are in the uniforms
6. on Friday - unclear if the assistant said on Friday or if he would finish on Friday
7. jumping up and down - means the restaurant is jumping up and down
8. that he had just caught - means the fisherman just caught the dock

Drill 2

1. Participle - Riding a unicycle, the clown amazed the students.
2. Infinitive - To sing the national anthem, you should memorize the lyrics beforehand.
3. Gerund - On entering the theater, I saw that the seats were all taken.
4. Infinitive - To catch a leprechaun, you need to correctly identify one.
5. Gerund - After running for hours, I noticed that the ground started to look blurry.
6. Participial - Standing on the chair, I could now reach the jar.

Drill 3

1. When I was only three years old, my mother was arrested.
2. If you get locked out of a car, Triple A can assist you.
3. While I was taking a shower, the fire alarm went off.
4. Though the lion was locked in a cage, the man was still afraid of it.
5. While I was sitting on a porch, the neighborhood seemed very calm.
6. If the test is too difficult, you can retake it another time.

Questions

1. Soggy with milk - it is a dangling element because he isn't soggy with milk. Corrected: He ate the delicious cookies that were soggy with milk.
2. To perform tests on animals - the animals aren't performing the tests. Corrected: To perform tests on animals, you should treat animals humanely.
3. without our costumes - there isn't a separate play without costumes. Corrected: After receiving some complaints from cast members, we rehearsed without our costumes for the play.
4. in my bedroom - ISIS probably isn't in his or her bedroom. Corrected: In my bedroom, I saw on television that the United States recently bombed ISIS.
5. N/A
6. nearly - since she was arrested, the criminal did not get away with the crime. Corrected: The criminal nearly got away with stealing my brand-new car, but she was arrested last night.

7. To make peanut butter and jelly - the first step doesn't make peanut butter and jelly. Corrected: To make peanut butter and jelly, you must start by putting two pieces of bread on your plate.
8. N/A
9. While designing a new website - it is a dangling element because an idea can't design a website. Corrected: While I was designing a new website, an idea popped into my head.
10. which hurt badly - it doesn't make sense for the ceiling to hurt badly. Corrected: Jumping up and down, I badly hurt my head by banging it into the ceiling.
11. Kicking and screaming - it makes more sense for the hysterical son to be kicking and screaming. Corrected: The mom dragged her hysterically kicking and screaming son out of the grocery store.
12. only - currently means that he or she only arrived (didn't sleep, walk, etc.) in Las Vegas. Corrected: Since I arrived in Las Vegas only late last night, I have not had time to see the surrounding area.
13. In the fish tank - it doesn't make sense for me to be in the fish tank. Corrected: I dropped into the fish tank some food for my fish.
14. which was unfortunately stained with ketchup - it doesn't make sense for a job interview to be stained with ketchup. Corrected: John wore a collared shirt, which was unfortunately stained with ketchup, to the job interview.
15. N/A
16. Walking for miles - it doesn't make sense for calves to walk. Corrected: Walking for miles, I felt as if my calves were grounded to a pulp.
17. only - because it is next to "arrived," only means Jake didn't do anything else to or with me. It makes more sense for the only to modify the after to mean that Jake didn't come before I called his mother. Corrected: My best friend, Jake, arrived to pick me up only after I frantically called his mother and told her to remind Jake that I needed a ride.
18. by overhearing my friends' conversation - Your friends' conversation didn't help Luke Skywalker destroy the Death Star. Corrected: By overhearing my friends' conversation, I learned that Luke Skywalker destroyed the Death Star.
19. To lift weights at our gym - The weights don't lift weights. Corrected: To lift weights at our gym, you need to clean the weights after each use.
20. on reusable plates - the people aren't on reusable plates. Corrected: To save money, the family decided to serve each other all of their food on reusable plates.

Parallel Structure

Diagnostic Test

For each sentence, determine whether it is parallel. If it isn't, make the necessary corrections.

1. The test is going to be difficult, time-consuming, and cover everything that was taught in class.

2. The hobbies I like above all are to paint portraits of celebrities and making my own wooden furniture.

3. When I retire, I want to eat bacon cheeseburgers, golf, and take multiple naps every day.

4. The dog was kicked by the baby, but the baby did not act out of malice.

5. I recommend that you either give me back my wallet or that you prepare for a fight.

6. By the time she turned thirty-three, several books were written by her.

7. In order to survive in the jungle, you not only need to have the right gear and tools but also know how to use them.

8. I plan first to learn how to use chopsticks and then eating at a Chinese restaurant.

9. By taking his time and because of his knowledge of the area, the army soldier was able to locate all of the landmines in the field.

10. He claims to be a saint, but he has fought neither evil nor saved anyone's life.

Parallel Structure

When writing, it is best to use parallel structure, which means keeping comparable things in the same grammatical form.

- Wrong/Not Parallel: swimming, burgers, and to take naps
- Parallel Gerunds: swimming, eating burgers, and taking naps
- Parallel Nouns: pools, burgers, and naps
- Parallel Infinitives: to swim, eat burgers, and take naps

Notice how *eating burgers* and *swimming* are parallel. Even though eating burgers is two words and swimming is one word, they are parallel because eating and swimming are gerunds, which are verbals ending in *-ing* and functioning as nouns.

Ignore words or phrases that modify the sentence element. The verb tense and voice, verbal type, and sentence element type should stay consistent.

- Parallel: The robber stole Jim's backpack and the phone. (Jim's backpack and the phone are parallel since backpack and phone are nouns)

- Parallel: I want to run and sit under the stars. (run and sit are parallel since run and sit are verbs in the same voice and tense)

Lists of things or attributes need to be parallel.

- Wrong: The bed is comfy, free of bugs, and it is also old.
- Parallel Adjectives: The bed is comfy, bug-free, and old.

- Wrong: The mayor was elected because he is hard-working and a veteran.
- Parallel Nouns: The mayor was elected because he is a hard worker and a veteran.

Drill 1 *Put the following words, phrases, and clauses into parallel groups.*

1. honesty, lying, to run, famous, wrestling, to dance, integrity, finite
2. John Jacobs, the man who likes to dance, over the rainbow, inside the house, snakes, pants on fire, without her, the cat in the hat
3. thick fog, benefactor, John ran to school, cereal for breakfast, I ate all of the cookies, lying to yourself, he sat, Oprah Winfrey

4. running for office, able to make a mistake, funny, sinking, stuck in the middle, scorched, watering my plant, strength
5. is smart, to live every day like there is no tomorrow, honestly, has millions of dollars, to fall in line, to cry, cares, quickly
6. cautious, mistake-prone, proves his ability to win tennis matches, fishing for compliments, the snakes were released, the science fair ended an hour ago, whining, increases the cost of a quality education

I. Parallel Structure for Conjunctions

Conjunctions are words used to join words, phrases, or clauses together while indicating their relationship.

- Mary-Kate *and* Ashley Olsen have starred in numerous films.
- She is *neither* stupid *nor* unattractive.
- I eat chocolate cake every day, *but* I don't gain weight.

There are three types of conjunctions: ***coordinating, correlative,*** and ***subordinating***.

Coordinating conjunctions join two sentence elements, whether they are subjects, objects, phrases, etc.

The coordinating conjunctions are: for   and   not   but   or   yet   so

Use parallel structure for comparable sentence elements connected with coordinating conjunction.

- My dog likes going on walks *and* ~~to meet~~ meeting new people.
- Frankie is handsome *but* ~~an idiot~~ stupid.
- Trisha went to the frat party, *but* her roommate ~~is staying~~ stayed in the dorm.
- Kelly and Kyle are having coffee *and* ~~eat~~ cookies.

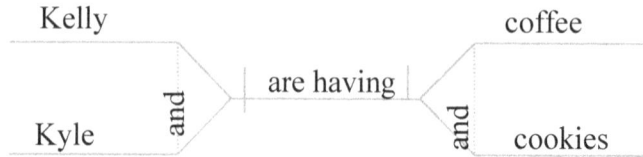

Drill 2 *Identify which subjects, clauses, and phrases need to be parallel. Next, identify whether the sentence is parallel. Repair all of the not-parallel sentences.*
1. Is he from Houston or Dallas?
2. I am sitting on the beach, but my friend stayed home.
3. The man sold my uncle and aunt a new sofa.
4. The bank teller told me to write my name on the back of each check, but I didn't listen.
5. Jill likes to dance all night and singing until she loses her voice.
6. I will win because of my determination and because I am smart.

Correlative conjunctions are always used in pairs. Some correlative conjunctions are:

both...and   whether...or   not only...but also   either...or   neither...nor

The sentence element in between the pair needs to have a parallel sentence element immediately after the pair.

- Neither the parents nor the students approved of the new teacher.
- Both Eliza and her sister are cheerleaders.
- Neither Mrs. Plunkett nor Mr. Redman buys fancy clothes or is tall and thin.

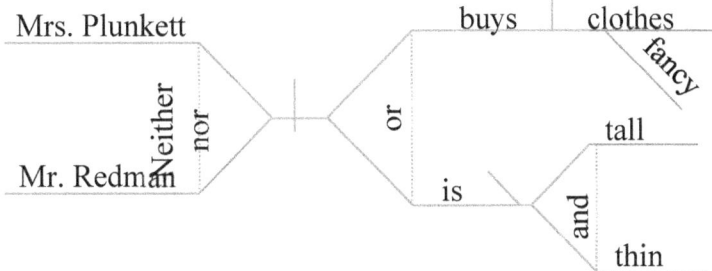

A sentence that isn't parallel can be fixed by moving the correlative conjunctions, adding or removing words, or rewriting the sentence.

- Not parallel: Mira will either cook chicken or tofu for dinner.
- Fixed: Mira will either cook chicken or cook tofu for dinner.
- Fixed: Mira will cook either chicken or tofu for dinner.
- Not parallel: Jake is not only wanted in Australia but also in New Zealand.
- Fixed: Jake is not only wanted in Australia but also wanted in New Zealand.
- Fixed: Jake is wanted not only in Australia but also in New Zealand.

Subordinating conjunctions are used to transition between two clauses. Consider the following examples:

- *If* I had known how to swim, I would have jumped into the pool and saved the drowning girl.
- I will attend the party *unless* you tell me not to come.

Common subordinating conjunctions include:

after	that	unless
although	once	until
as	provided	when
because	that	whenever
before	rather than	where
even if	since	whereas
even	so that	wherever
though	than	while
if	that	why
in order	though	

Comparable elements across subordinating conjunctions should be parallel. Consider the following examples:

- Wrong: Once I learn swimming, I want to learn how to pilot a boat.
- Corrected: Once I learn how to swim, I want to learn how to pilot a boat.

Drill 3 *Identify whether the sentence is parallel. Repair all of the not parallel sentences.*

1. I will find you whether you are running away or hiding in someone's house.
2. Arsenic is not only an element but also poisonous.
3. Either you must sleep or drink fluids to feel better.
4. Neither John nor my new friend is able to help me with my math homework.
5. A square needs to have both equal side lengths and also have equal angle measurements.
6. George not only stole my wallet but also my car keys.

II. Parallel Structure for Voice

The *active voice* is used to describe a sentence in which the subject executes the action expressed in the verb. If there is a direct object, it receives this action.

- The cat is pouncing.
- The boy ate all of his ice cream.
- The girl reads many books.
- I will run to the end of the block.

The *passive voice* is used when the subject is the recipient of the action expressed in the verb. Often, it is used to emphasize this recipient. There is never a direct object in a passive-voice sentence. In fact, the noun that might function as the direct object in an active sentence becomes the subject in a passive sentence.

- All the ice cream <u>was eaten</u> by one boy.
- *Harry Potter* <u>was written</u> by J. K. Rowling.
- The house <u>was finished</u>.
- Dinner <u>is being made</u> as we speak.

Notice in the passive sentences that *by* appears or is implied with each passive verb. *By* describes who or what is/was actually doing the action. It is fairly easy to change a passive sentence to an active one by simply switching the word order.

<u>**Passive**</u>		<u>**Active**</u>
All the ice cream was eaten by one boy.	→	The boy ate all the ice cream.
Harry Potter was written by J. K. Rowling.	→	J. K. Rowling wrote *Harry Potter*.
The house was finished.	→	They finished the house.

Parallel sentence elements should use the same voice. Consider the following sentences and how they can be fixed by changing to active voice.

- Wrong: I practiced dribbling a basketball, and then several free throws were shot by me.
- Fixed: I practiced dribbling a basketball and then shot several free throws.
- Wrong: The moon was jumped over by the cow, and then the cow landed back on Earth.
- Fixed: The cow jumped over the moon and then landed back on Earth.

Drill 4 *Make the sentences parallel by changing everything to active voice.*

1. The roof was repaired by the construction worker, and then the construction worker went home.
2. The teenager stayed out past her curfew after several beer cans were consumed by her.
3. The window was broken by teenagers, but they admitted responsibility and paid the repair cost.
4. The table was flipped by the angry customer, and then he threatened to sue the company.
5. My dog ran outside, but decided to come back after several neighbors were frightened by her.
6. A mouse was almost eaten by a cat, but the cat decided to let the mouse go.

III. Improper Comparisons

Improper comparisons are significant issues that make the thinking in a sentence unclear and that this book has placed as a subset of this section that deals with parallel structure.

Diagnostic Test

Repair each sentence that uses improper comparisons.

1. I think that Kevin Hart is funnier than anyone in the world.

2. My favorite Thai dish, pad thai, is as delicious and far more popular than any French dish.

3. Superman, whose only weakness is kryptonite, is stronger than any superhero.

4. My older brother is smarter than anyone else in my sixth-grade science class.

5. I think that the best basketball player is Steph Curry, because his three-point shooting is as quick as and more efficient than any other basketball player.

6. I love Boston because it has as much a love of sports as I do.

7. I think that Harvard's code of conduct is far more reasonable than Yale.

8. No other baseball team has accomplished so much as the New York Yankees.

9. *Hamlet*, written by William Shakespeare in 1602, is just as interesting and far better written than *Fifty Shades of Grey*.

10. I like reading books and imagining the action more than to sit and watch a movie and be told what happens.

A. Compare the right things

Make sure to compare the right things. Comparing my dog to you is different from comparing my dog to your dog. Compare people's traits, possessions, actions, and accomplishments to people's traits, possessions, actions, and accomplishments.

Examples: Wrong: My taste in music is better than Mike.
Fixed: My taste in music is better than Mike's.

Wrong: I scored higher on the test than your score.

Fixed: I scored higher on the test than you.

Drill 1 *Fix each comparison that compares the wrong things.*
1. I think I should be the point guard, because my passing is better than anyone else.
2. It is even colder in Antarctica than it is inside your refrigerator.
3. John swam faster than my personal best time.
4. My favorite song requires fewer instruments than your.
5. My ability to land on my feet after being airborne is why I am better at skiing than you are.
6. I always wanted to be a doctor, but my determination was never as strong as Dr. Smith.

B. Elliptical clauses

An **elliptical clause** is one in which one or more words have been left out, because the reader can infer what the missing words are.

Consider the example from "Compare the right things": *I scored higher on the test than you.* In this example, *you* is an elliptical clause because it is implied that I scored higher on the test than you did. Similarly, in the comparison *my taste in music is better than Mike's*, it is implied that my taste in music is better than Mike's taste in music.

These types of clauses often occur in comparisons and are grammatically correct.

C. Don't be better than yourself

It doesn't make sense for something to be better than itself. Therefore, don't write that something is better or worse at something than each member of a group that includes itself. Instead, write that the thing is better than **any other** member of the group. Likewise, for a person, write that he or she is better than anyone **else** in the group.

Examples: Wrong: I am smarter than everyone in my math class. (Incorrectly states that I am smarter than myself)
Fixed: I am smarter than everyone **else** in my math class.

Wrong: I would rather go to Tokyo than go to any city in the world. (Incorrectly states that Tokyo isn't a city or that I would rather go to Tokyo than go to Tokyo)
Fixed: I would rather go to Tokyo than go to any **other** city in the world.

Don't include an *else* or *only* if nothing needs to be excluded.

Examples: Wrong: Albert Einstein is smarter than everyone **else** in my math class. (Wrongly implies that Albert Einstein is in my math class)

Fixed: Albert Einstein is smarter than everyone in my math class.

Wrong: I would rather go to Tokyo than any **other** city in the United States. (The *other* is unclear and confusing since Tokyo isn't in the United States)

Fixed: I would rather go to Tokyo than any city in the United States.

Drill 2 *Fix each improper comparison.*
1. My goal was to score higher on the final exam than anyone.
2. My favorite comedy movie, *Dumb and Dumber*, is funnier than every horror movie.
3. I think that the town I grew up in is safer than any other city.
4. My favorite type of fish swims faster than any other type of fish does.
5. The class clown is funnier than anyone in our school.
6. I think that it is more difficult to learn rocket science than anything.

D. As ... as

As ... as is used to make comparisons dealing with the extent of something. Never leave out or replace the first or second as.

Examples: Wrong: I was *as* smart and more creative than any student in the class.
Fixed: I was *as* smart *as* and more creative than any student in the class.

Wrong: No player has done so much for baseball *as* Jackie Robinson.
Fixed: No player has done *as* much for baseball *as* Jackie Robinson.

A single *as* can be used as a conjunction or preposition.

Examples: I leaned forward *as* I caught the ball. (conjunction)
I wish I could do *as* I please. (conjunction)
The old man couldn't remember his life *as* an infant. (preposition)
As a lifeguard, he knew it was his duty to save the drowning boy. (preposition)

Drill 3 *Repair each sentence that misuses as ... as comparisons.*
1. Much as I wanted to be at the party, I still need to finish my homework.
2. My father, Harry Karl, told me to do so much studying as I needed to do in order to ace my finals.
3. As a teacher, I had a different perspective on why students didn't do as well as they could.
4. I think that the President has as much stardom and more power than any other citizen of the United States.
5. No basketball player has made so many three pointers as Ray Allen.
6. His monster drawing looked as scary and far more realistic than any of the other Halloween drawings.

Improper Comparison Exercises

Repair each sentence that uses improper comparisons.

1. I think that vampires are far more interesting and as scary as any creature.

2. My office building is far better equipped to handle severe earthquakes than any of the other neighboring buildings.

3. Much as I tried to prepare for the final exam, I couldn't understand the more difficult concepts.

4. I am more excited about swimming in the pool than about the arcade.

5. I found that John's poker face was as difficult to read as professional poker players.

6. He painted portraits of flowers that looked as realistic as any other photographs.

7. I have never wanted to eat a piece of bread so much as I did during my day of fasting.

8. The mushrooms in our store are as fresh as, if not better than, any others.

9. My roommate is taller than anybody in his class.

10. I find that Emily Dickinson's poems are better written than Robert Frost.

11. I find African art to be as colorful and far more moving than American art.

12. The Boston Museum of Science has more fascinating exhibits than any museum in Massachusetts.

13. My best friend, John Smith, is funnier than anyone in his grade.

14. I was surprised to learn that my average golf score was lower than Charles Barkley.

15. New York City is as lively and far more populated than any other U.S. city.

Parallel Structure Exercises

For each sentence, determine whether it is parallel. If the sentence is not parallel, make the necessary corrections.

1. Eating healthful foods and training multiple hours a day with proper coaching made the athlete into a superstar.
2. My brother visiting France, able to speak French and with enough money to do whatever he wanted, felt right at home.
3. Adolf Hitler was very dangerous because he had the ability to lead others and of convincing them to do terrible things.
4. The man sang ever so beautifully and with passion.
5. Preparing as best as he could, the tennis player's training regimen included running ten miles per day, watching the best tennis players in the world, and a good luck charm.
6. In order to stay under the family budget, my mother not only is cutting down on her trips to the salon, but she is also buying cheaper foods.
7. Understanding American history, farming, and being an experienced drawer, John was the perfect artist to paint American farms from the 19th century.
8. The new manager proved herself to be not only strategic and efficient, but also a woman capable of befriending anyone.
9. The woman is believed to be a witch because she stays up late, is very traditional, and her daughter isn't loved by her.
10. The chemical can be used for laundry detergent, dish detergent, and as a shoe polisher.
11. The fewer people that are infected with the disease, there are fewer people that can transmit it to others.
12. Humans are innately capable of learning new languages and how to walk.
13. The teacher told the students to study hard, do their homework, and that they should expect a quiz after the school break.
14. I am not only afraid of the dark but also of spiders.
15. I went to the school dance hoping to find a dance partner, but with fear of asking someone to dance.

Parallel Structure Exercises

For each sentence, determine whether it is parallel. If it isn't, make the necessary corrections.

16. Bill Gates officially established Microsoft in 1975, and it was transformed through decades into a billion-dollar company.
17. My friend Mary is very unique: she is a magician, an Olympian, and she has only nine fingers.
18. When I die, I hope to be remembered because I want others to remember my teachings and also because of my desire to have made a difference in the world.
19. I was stung by a bee, but it died immediately afterwards.
20. The boxer punched me ever so powerfully and with quickness.
21. These exercises neither should be difficult nor time-consuming.
22. Thomas Edison was a legend: he invented light bulbs, phonographs, and never stopped learning.
23. The fly was swatted by the man, but the man feared that it would fly away unscathed.
24. I suggest that you neither get in a fight with the bully nor that you prank him.
25. We will win the war because of our determination and because we fight for a righteous cause.
26. I want to be able to run at supersonic speeds, fly, and be invisible.
27. He believed that he could defeat cancer by going to church, which was an hour away, and praying multiple hours a day.
28. Major League Baseball general managers attempt to evaluate how much players are worth, and thus determining which trade offers to make, accept, and reject.
29. I will not go to the restaurant without you and unless we go on a Friday night.
30. A waitress at our restaurant typically makes fifteen dollars an hour for merely taking orders from customers and then to give the orders to the chefs.

Answers

Parallel Structure Diagnostic

1. Not parallel - The test is going to be difficult, time-consuming, and all-encompassing.
2. Not parallel - The hobbies I like above all are painting portraits of celebrities and making my own wooden furniture.
3. Parallel
4. Not parallel- The baby kicked the dog, but did not act out of malice.
5. Not parallel - I recommend that you either give me back my wallet or prepare for a fight.
6. Not parallel - By the time she turned thirty-three, she had written several books.
7. Not parallel - In order to survive in the jungle, you need to not only have the right gear and tools but also know how to use them.
8. Not parallel - I plan first to learn how to use chopsticks and then to eat at a Chinese restaurant.
9. Not parallel - By taking his time and knowing the area, the army soldier was able to locate all of the landmines in the field.
10. Not parallel - He claims to be a saint, but he has neither fought evil nor saved anyone's life.

Improper Comparison Diagnostic

1. I think that Kevin Hart is funnier than anyone **else** in the world.
2. My favorite Thai dish, pad thai, is as delicious **as** and far more popular than any French dish.
3. Superman, whose only weakness is kryptonite, is stronger than any **other** superhero.
4. My older brother is smarter than anyone ~~else~~ in my sixth-grade science class.
5. I think that the best basketball player is Steph Curry, because his three-point shooting is as quick as and more efficient than any other basketball player**'s**.
6. N/A
7. I think that Harvard's code of conduct is far more reasonable than Yale**'s**.
8. No other baseball team has accomplished **as** much as the New York Yankees.
9. *Hamlet*, written by William Shakespeare in 1602, is just as interesting **as** and far better written than *Fifty Shades of Grey*.
10. I like reading books and imagining the action more than **sitting** and **watching** a movie and **being** told what happens.

Parallel Structure Drill 1

1. (honesty, integrity) (lying, wrestling) (to run, to dance) (famous, finite)
2. (John Jacobs, the man who likes to dance, snakes, pants on fire, the cat in the hat) (over the rainbow, inside the house, without her)
3. (thick fog, benefactor, cereal for breakfast, Oprah Winfrey) (John ran to school, I ate all of the cookies, he sat) (lying to yourself)
4. (running for office, watering my plant, sinking) (able to make a mistake, funny, stuck in the middle, scorched) (strength)
5. (is smart, has millions of dollars, cares) (to live every day like there is no tomorrow, to fall in line, to cry) (honestly, quickly)
6. (cautious, mistake-prone) (proves his ability to win tennis matches,

increases the cost of a quality education) (fishing for compliments, whining) (the snakes were released, the science fair ended an hour ago)

Parallel Structure Drill 2

1. Houston and Dallas need to be parallel. The sentence is parallel.
2. I am sitting and my friend stayed need to be parallel. The sentence is not parallel. I am sitting on the beach, but my friend is staying home.
3. uncle and aunt need to be parallel. The sentence is parallel.
4. bank teller told and I didn't need to be parallel. The sentence is parallel.
5. to dance and singing need to be parallel. The sentence is not parallel. Jill likes dancing all night and singing until she loses her voice.
6. determination and because I am smart need to be parallel. The sentence is not parallel. I will win because I am determined and smart.

Parallel Structure Drill 3

1. Parallel
2. Not parallel - Arsenic is not only an element but also a poison.
3. Not parallel - You must either sleep or drink fluids to feel better.
4. Parallel
5. Not parallel - A square needs to have both equal side lengths and equal angle measurements.
6. Not parallel - George stole not only my wallet but also my car keys.

Parallel Structure Drill 4

1. The construction worker repaired the roof and then went home.
2. The teenager stayed out past her curfew after she consumed several beer cans.
3. The teenagers broke the window, but they admitted responsibility and paid the repair cost.
4. The angry customer flipped the table and then threatened to sue the company.
5. My dog ran outside, but decided to come back after she frightened several neighbors.
6. A cat almost ate a mouse, but decided to let it go.

Improper Comparison Drill 1

1. I think I should be the point guard, because my passing is better than anyone else**'s**.
2. N/A
3. John swam faster than **I ever have**.
4. My favorite song requires fewer instruments than your**s**.
5. N/A
6. I always wanted to be a doctor, but my determination was never as strong as Dr. Smith**'s**.

Improper Comparison Drill 2

1. My goal was to score higher on the final exam than anyone **else**.
2. N/A
3. I think that the town I grew up in is safer than any ~~other~~ city.
4. N/A
5. The class clown is funnier than anyone **else** in our school.
6. I think that it is more difficult to learn rocket science than **to learn** anything **else**.

Improper Comparison Drill 3

1. **As much** as I wanted to be at the party, I still need to finish my homework.
2. My father, Harry Karl, told me to do **as** much studying as I needed to do in order to ace my finals.
3. N/A
4. I think that the President has as much stardom **as** and more power than any other citizen of the United States.
5. No basketball player has made **as** many three pointers as Ray Allen.
6. His monster drawing looked as scary **as** and far more realistic than any of the other Halloween drawings.

Improper Comparison Exercises

1. I think that vampires are far more interesting and as scary as any **other** creature.
2. My office building is far better equipped to handle severe earthquakes than any of the ~~other~~ neighboring buildings.
3. **As much** as I tried to prepare for the final exam, I couldn't understand the more difficult concepts.
4. I am more excited about swimming in the pool than about **playing in** the arcade.
5. I found that John's poker face was as difficult to read as professional poker players**'**.
6. He painted portraits of flowers that looked as realistic as any ~~other~~ photographs.
7. I have never wanted to eat a piece of bread **as** much as I did during my day of fasting.
8. N/A
9. My roommate is taller than anybody **else** in his class.
10. I find that Emily Dickinson's poems are better written than Robert Frost**'s**.
11. I find African art to be as colorful **as** and far more moving than American art.
12. The Boston Museum of Science has more fascinating exhibits than any **other** museum in Massachusetts.
13. My best friend, John Smith, is funnier than anyone **else** in his grade.
14. I was surprised to learn that my average golf score was lower than Charles Barkley**'s**.
15. New York City is as lively **as** and far more populated than any other U.S. city.

Parallel Structure Exercises

1. Parallel
2. Not parallel - My brother visiting France, with the ability to speak French and with enough money to do whatever he wanted, felt right at home.
3. Not parallel - Adolf Hitler was very dangerous because he had the ability to lead others and to convince them to do terrible things.
4. Not parallel - The man sang ever so beautifully and passionately.
5. Not parallel - Preparing as best as he could, the tennis player's training regimen included running ten miles per day, watching the best tennis players in the world, and wearing a good luck charm.
6. Not parallel - In order to stay under the family budget, my mother not only is cutting down on her trips to the salon, but also is buying cheaper foods.
7. Not parallel - Understanding American history, farming, and the art of drawing, John was the perfect artist to paint American farms from the 19th century.
8. Not parallel - The new manager proved herself to be not only strategic and efficient, but also capable of befriending anyone.
9. Not parallel - The woman is believed to be a witch because she stays up late, is very traditional, and doesn't love her daughter.
10. Not parallel - The chemical can be used for laundry detergent, dish detergent, and shoe polishers.
11. Not parallel - The fewer people that are infected with the disease, the fewer people that can transmit it to others.
12. Parallel
13. Not parallel - The teacher told the students to study hard, do their homework, and expect a quiz after the school break.
14. Not parallel - I am afraid not only of the dark but also of spiders.
15. Not parallel - I went to the school dance with hope of finding a dance partner, but with fear of asking someone to dance.
16. Not parallel - Microsoft was officially established by Bill Gates in 1975, and it was transformed through decades into a billion-dollar company.
17. Not parallel - My friend Mary is very unique: she is a magician, she is an Olympian, and she has only nine fingers.
18. Not parallel - When I die, I hope to be remembered because I want others to remember my teachings and I desire to have made a difference in the world.
19. Not parallel - A bee stung me, but it died immediately afterwards.
20. Not parallel - The boxer punched me ever so powerfully and quickly.
21. Not parallel - These exercises should be neither difficult nor time-consuming.
22. Not parallel - Thomas Edison was a legend: he invented light bulbs and phonographs, and he never stopped learning.
23. Not parallel - The man swatted the fly, but feared that it would fly away unscathed.
24. Not parallel - I suggest that you neither get in a fight with the bully nor prank him.
25. Not parallel - We will win the war because we are determined and fight for a righteous cause.
26. Parallel
27. Parallel

28. Not parallel - Major League Baseball general managers attempt to evaluate how much players are worth, and thus determine which trade offers to make, accept, and reject.
29. Not parallel - I will only go to the restaurant with you and on a Friday night.
30. Not parallel - A waitress at our restaurant typically makes fifteen dollars an hour for merely taking orders from customers and then giving the orders to the chefs.

Second Cumulative Review

For each sentence, determine whether it is grammatically correct. If it is grammatically incorrect, identify the type of error:

Verb - V   Subject Verb Agreement - A   Pronoun - P   Fragment - F

Misplaced Modifier - M   Lack of Parallel Structure - L

(V, A, P, F, M, L)

*Improper comparisons are part of Lack of Parallel Structure

1. After hosting an extravagant birthday party, six dollars and eighteen cents were all that I had in my bank account.

2. Talking to the man beside me, I realized the importance of good posture, a strong handshake, and a friendly smile.

3. To raise my test scores, I almost studied for four hours: more than anyone else in my class.

4. My brother, sitting on the sofa, is smarter than everyone in my family.

5. My favorite thing to do in Boston is either to kayak on the Charles River or watching Red Sox games at Fenway Park.

6. Is it her who I should promote to manager?

7. Representative Johnson is the member of the State House whom I think can best lead the new committee.

8. Alexander Hamilton had very clear ambitions for the young United States. To establish an effective centralized state with modern economic and banking capabilities.

9. The movie *Titanic*, directed by James Cameron, received as much acclaim and more Oscars than any other movie from 1997.

10. Upon entering the school, I realized that I either forgot my books or my lunch.

11. Upon arriving at the gate of the mansion, I was told that I needed an appointment in order to speak to one of its inhabitants, my best friend from high school.

12. To help me learn algebra, my teacher gave me a worksheet, which was filled with challenging word problems.

13. While confidently running through the obstacle course, a single rock caused me to slip and fall on my face.

14. It is never wise to administer quick judgement upon someone for his mistakes. Because one might not be aware of hardships or circumstances that someone might be facing in his private life.

15. No scientist has done so much to inspire me as Albert Einstein, who developed the theory of relativity

16. The jury, even after a lengthy period of deliberating among themselves, was finding it difficult to deliver their verdict on the high-profile case.

17. Not only the cheerleaders but also the coach is planning to attend my brother's funeral, which will start at noon.

18. I want a friend who is always willing to try new things and isn't afraid of being herself.

19. It seemed like the entire class was invited except for he and I.

20. Fewer students from the affluent suburb are being admitted to the most competitive colleges, partly because veteran teachers at the high school are retiring and younger less experienced teachers will take their place.

21. The muscular man gave me a cup of coffee in his tight-fitting uniform.

22. I made a new best friend who is not only funny but also helps me with my math homework.

23. The woman with all the money, clothing and expensive jewels, go shopping on a weekly basis in this affluent and gentrified area.

24. In order to get where I wanted to go, I took a long ride to a distant island on a private helicopter.

25. Much to the dismay of students everywhere, who are now faced with largely unappealing lunch options. Michelle Obama implemented in public schools new health and nutrition standards for food.

26. My brother thought that he was a better basketball player than everyone in his school.

27. Absolutely none of the students, including John and I, have access to the teacher's lounge.

28. Singing in the shower, the walls were so thin that everyone could hear me.

29. The parents were completely blindsided. When the group of academically successful and well reputed students were apprehended by the police at the lake house party for underage drinking. The students' futures took a turn for the worst.

30. The English statesman Edmund Burke is often assumed to have initiated modern conservatism, but the Austrian diplomat Klemens von Metternich had promoted similar ideas throughout Europe during the same time period.

31. I believe that humans are either programmed to search for life's meaning, or we are just here to have a good time.

32. The herds of consumers, both insatiable and exploitable, flocks towards the Apple store with great anticipation and excitement.

33. I gave some chocolate chip cookies to my mom that I made myself.

34. Even though America's Founding Fathers were not familiar with the technological progress or comfortable lifestyles that we enjoy today, they were pioneering the establishment of political systems that are still used in modern society today.

35. I called customer service, but I hung up after almost waiting for three hours.

36. In a capitalist economy, everyone must put their best effort forward to provide some good or service in exchange for money or assets.

37. Anyone involved in the formation of the union could have their contract terminated.

38. Training recruits over the years, the drill sergeant became adept at detecting soldiers who have been shirking their exercises or avoiding responsibilities.

39. There has been numerous instances of religious violence throughout history.

40. My best friend, Jake, loves baking chocolate chip cookies and to pretend to be a celebrity.

41. Swimming in the pool, my bathing suit started to slip off, but no one noticed.

42. People sometimes question the legitimacy of many politicians' net savings and income sources. Which somehow accumulate to millions of dollars over spans of merely six or seven years.

43. The man thinks he is amazing, but he has won neither any awards nor done anything remarkable.

44. To get a perfect score on the test, minor details should not be ignored.

45. It is up to we survivors to maintain some societal order despite this zombie outbreak!

46. The central computer, along with all of the mobile devices in the state building, were temporarily disabled by the EMP attack.

47. Depending on how rigorous the program in which enrollees earn their degree, students with public school backgrounds are as likely to do well in their chosen careers as students will with private school backgrounds.

48. A modern author such as A.K. Rawlings, who writes for brainy boys in fourth grade, differs from previous times in her themes, her approach, and her style.

49. Despite receiving some complaints, my criterion for selecting students has never changed.

50. My phone, which I had bought last week, was stolen by a robber, but the robber did not take my wallet.

51. Early 20th century Europe experienced an emerging set of conflicting ideologies commonly known as the "isms." Comprised mainly of nationalism, classical liberalism, socialism, and Marxism.

52. If only the applicant had continued her studying for the LSAT, she may have raised her test scores and gained admission to the prestigious law school.

53. Although Ben Jonson's plays are classics of the Elizabethan stage, popular for their well-constructed plots, engaging characters, and memorable, witty lines that resounded throughout the Globe Theater where they were performed, nevertheless, they still do not rise to the same level of genius as Shakespeare.

54. In a utilitarian sense, public school educators work diligently to find the optimal settings to foster the best learning experience for the greatest number of students. A seemingly unachievable balance somewhere in between testing and instruction.

55. Yanis Varoufakis was one of those politicians who wears unorthodox outfits in order to make a statement.

56. The preparations for the surprise birthday party began when everyone in the room was ordered to hide themselves among the furniture.

57. Searching for hours for the car keys, I only found them after I remembered to check my pockets.

58. Onto the foreground of the ceremony arrives the President and the Secretary of State.

59. The secretary, who sits at the desk at the far end of the waiting room and greets people who enter the doctor's office, believes that the new patient has forwarded to her yesterday the patient's records.

60. Although at the conclusion to the original version of *Great Expectations* Pip and Estella seem to drift apart, Dickens, upon the urging of his fellow authors, altered the last paragraph of the novel so as to make the relationship between Pip and Estella seem to lead in a positive direction.

61. The boy in the bright yellow uniform gave a piece of pizza to the teacher that was slightly burnt.

62. The people whom were a part of the Roosevelt Administration are well known for their role in helping America during the Great Depression.

63. The snake oil salesman told me that his mystery potion could be used for cleaning, polishing, and to kill bugs.

64. Despite winning the state primary, my brother is malicious and an idiot.

65. My grandfather was a remarkable man: he never cheated, always tried his best, and he saved many lives.

66. Students who have been both ambitious and diligent know that the best time to prepare for final exams is now.

67. With an acceptance rate in 2018 of only thirteen percent of its applicants, Phillips Andover is now considered more challenging to be admitted to than any prep school in the country.

68. Unlike the music of Beethoven, Wagner tends to compose with lines that seem to float on beyond what the listeners would expect to be their conclusions.

69. Jane borrowed my pencil without asking me, which I planned to use to take notes.

70. I darted past defenders who were blocking my way to the basketball hoop, until a basket was scored by me.

71. Sporting their new uniforms and helmets and warming up with vigorous nonstop calisthenics, the team are hoping that they are ready at kickoff to show their fans that they are a team to be proud of.

72. With our backpacks we hiked all afternoon through Harold Parker State Forest and return home only at dusk.

73. When free markets are unleashed. The forces of competition increase the quality of life for the vast majority of the population and an abundance of constantly improving innovations becomes apparent.

74. To get to the train on time, I made sure to pack my bag, lunch, and leave early.

75. To help students prepare for tests, flash cards are extremely useful.

76. With its population of over eight million inhabitants, London is larger than any other city in the United Kingdom.

77. At the rally, in front of thousands of his supporters, he listed the achievements he has four years ago said he would achieve.

78. The President and the Attorney General sat discussing the policy in the Oval Office.

79. The ideas behind a Green New Deal as proposed by Alexandra Ocasio Cortez are more radical than her rivals, even the socialist Bernie Sanders.

80. Coach told John quickly to run to the locker room to get his cleats.

Second Cumulative Review Answers

Answers may vary.

1. M - "six dollars and eighteen cents" didn't host the birthday party, the speaker did

2. Correct

3. M - the speaker didn't "almost study," he studied for almost "four hours"

4. L - smarter than everyone else

5. L - to kayak is not parallel to watching

6. P - Is it she

7. P - who I think

8. F - second cluster of words is an incomplete thought

9. L - The as ... as comparison "received as much acclaim" is missing the second as

10. L - Forgot my books isn't parallel to my lunch

11. Correct

12. Correct

13. M - the rock was not "confidently running through the obstacle course"

14. F - second cluster of words is an incomplete thought

15. Correct

16. A - themselves... were finding it

17. Correct

18. Correct

19. P - me and him

20. V - teachers are taking their place

21. M - the cup of coffee was not wearing a "tight fitting uniform"

22. *L - funny is not parallel to helps me*

23. *A - the woman... goes*

24. *M - the distant island is not "on a private helicopter"*

25. *F - first cluster of words is an incomplete thought*

26. *L - than everyone else*

27. *P - including John and me*

28. *M - the walls weren't singing in the shower*

29. *F - second cluster of words is an incomplete thought*

30. *Correct*

31. *L - Programmed to search for life's meaning is not parallel to we are just here to have a good time*

32. *A - herds... flock*

33. *M - the speaker did not make his mom himself*

34. *V - they pioneered the establishment of political systems*

35. *M - "almost" should be next to three hours and not waiting*

36. *P - everyone... his or her best effort forward*

37. *P - anyone... his or her contract*

38. *V - soldiers who had been shirking*

39. *A - there have been... instances*

40. *L - To pretend isn't parallel to baking*

41. *M - the bathing suit was not "swimming in the pool"*

42. *F - the second cluster of words is an incomplete thought*

43. *L - any awards is not parallel to done anything remarkable*

44. M - minor details are not getting "a perfect score on the test"

45. P - us survivors

46. A - the central computer… was

47. Correct

48. L - differs from the works of previous times

49. M - my criterion was not "receiving some complaints"

50. L - mix of active and passive voice

51. F - the second cluster of words is an incomplete thought

52. V - she could have raised

53. L - "Ben Jonson's plays" are not parallel to "Shakespeare"

54. F - the second cluster of words is an incomplete thought

55. A - politicians who wear

56. P - everyone… himself

57. M - only should be next to after and not found

58. A - arrive… the President and the Secretary of State

59. V - the new patient forwarded to her yesterday

60. Correct

61. M - the teacher was not slightly burnt

62. P - the people who

63. L - "to kill bugs" is not parallel to "polishing"

64. L - "malicious" is not parallel to "idiot"

65. L - "always tried his best" is not parallel to "he saved many lives"

66. Correct

67. L - *than any other prep school*

68. L - *"the music of Beethoven" is not parallel to "Wagner"*

69. M - *"which I planned to use to take notes" should be next to my pencil and not me*

70. L - *mix of active and passive*

71. *Correct*

72. V - *returned home only at dusk*

73. F - *the second cluster of words is an incomplete thought*

74. L - *"lunch" is not parallel to "leave early"*

75. *Correct*

76. *Correct*

77. V - *listed the achievements he four years ago had said*

78. M - *the "policy" is not related to the "Oval Office"*

79. L - *more radical than the ideas of her rivals*

80. M - *"quickly" should be after "run"*

USAGE

The customary way in which words are used and understood within the English-speaking community: punctuation with commas where we pause; periods where we stop; diction to choose with care, apropos, not wordy.

Punctuation

Diagnostic Test

Determine if the sentence is grammatically correct. Correct all errors.

1. The tests this semester have been: difficult, time-consuming, and unpredictable.

2. Before his big race, Usain Bolt ate some chicken nuggets—the breakfast of champions.

3. Emily told me, "my favorite song is 'Stairway to Heaven.'"

4. John is my best friend, however, I don't always treat him as well as I should.

5. The secret to making a big, tasty apple pie: apply butter liberally.

6. Between September 4, 2017, and December 10, 2017, I lost $13,167 on FanDuel; nevertheless, I haven't stopped playing.

7. My brother shouted, "Samantha took all of my candy"; in reality, he just forgot that he had eaten all of his candy.

8. The best time to wear a striped sweater is all the time: winter, spring, summer, and fall.

9. Waiting for the bus to arrive I played video games on my phone—I didn't see the bus until it drove past me.

10. The bus driver made an announcement, "This is the final stop."

Punctuation

"I said stop!"

I. Commas ,

A. Review: Run-on Sentences and Nonrestrictive Elements

Recall that commas can't be used to separate two complete sentences.

Examples: Wrong: I like to swim, Sally likes to go shopping.

Wrong: I have a flight tomorrow morning, I need to go to bed early.

Also, nonrestrictive elements are separated by commas from the rest of the sentence. Restrictive elements are not separated by commas.

Examples: Jack Johnson, singing from the stage, attracted an enormous crowd.

Jack Johnson is the man singing from the stage.

B. Introductory Phrase or Clause

Commas are placed after dependent clauses or modifying phrases that begin a sentence.

Examples: Although I wanted to attend the concert, I couldn't make it because I got into a car accident.

In middle school, my daughter attended only half of her classes.

Drill 1 *Punctuate the following.*
1. The success of *Breaking Bad* a TV show produced by Vince Gilligan demonstrates American audiences' fascination with drugs and violence.
2. Even after seven years no one has found my wife's murderer moreover there aren't any suspects.
3. The teacher whom I like more than any other is Linda Parker who is patient and kind.
4. The family pet kitten Paws loved scratching the walls which looked like they belonged on the set of a Wolverine movie.

5. Sarah and Rebecca went to the library to study for their upcoming biology test I stayed home and watched *Footloose*.
6. In college my girlfriend and I had practiced about twenty times for the play nevertheless we both forgot our lines during the premiere.

C. Joining Independent Clauses

Commas are placed between most independent clauses joined with a coordinating conjunction such as *and* or *but*.

Examples: The man was wearing a Rolex, and he asked me to spare him some change.

I ran as fast as I could, but I didn't make it to class on time.

For closely connected short independent clauses, the comma may be omitted.

Example: Correct: I like swimming, but Sally likes shopping.

Correct: I like swimming but Sally likes shopping.

D. List

Commas separate items in lists with three or more.

Examples: My favorite things to do are eating burgers, swimming in pools, and going shopping.

Participation trophies are meant to reward effort, perseverance, and sportsmanship.

E. Pairs of Adjectives

Separate the adjectives with commas if the order of the adjectives doesn't matter

Examples: I met a *tall, handsome* man. (handsome, tall man means the same thing when reversed)

I picked up a *heavy, bulky* box. (bulky, heavy box means the same thing when reversed)

Don't use commas if the order does matter.

Examples: I threw the *useless participation* trophy in the trash. (participation useless trophy doesn't mean the same thing)

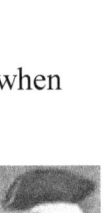

I picked up a *heavy blue* box. (blue heavy box is awkward because blue box is a type of box)

Drill 2 *Punctuate the following.*
1. The large fast kangaroo jumped over my head when I was asleep.
2. I went to the White House to meet President Trump but he was too busy to speak to me.
3. My least favorite movies are *Clueless The Godfather* and *Ocean's 8*.
4. I took a long deep breath and then I shot the bright orange basketball into the hoop.
5. John picked up a small green wallet but he didn't know whether to keep it give it to the police or ask someone nearby whether it belonged to him.
6. I want to learn how to swim without a life jacket but I am too afraid of drowning or getting attacked by sharks.

II. Colons :

The colon must be preceded by an independent clause. What comes after the colon explains or illustrates this complete sentence.

Examples: I want a friend who can do the following: keep secrets, tell funny jokes, and respect my boundaries.

   I know what to do: study.

As seen in the previous two examples, colons can introduce a list of one or more things. Clauses can follow colons if they explain or illustrate the preceding independent clause.

Examples: The cashier had a good reason to quit: his boss threatened to kill him after the cashier mischarged a customer.

   I was astonished: I didn't even know that it was possible to perform such a feat.

Colons can be used to separate a quotation from a complete thought that introduces it.

Examples: Maya Angelou understood the importance of loving what you do: "You can only become truly accomplished at something you love."

   Denzel Washington doesn't care about trophies: "My mother used to tell me, man gives the award, God gives the reward. I don't need another plaque."

Don't use a colon if the sentence makes sense without it.

Example: Wrong: My favorite movies include: *The Dark Knight* and *Mean Girls*.

   Fixed: My favorite moves include *The Dark Knight* and *Mean Girls*.

III. Semicolons ;

Semicolons must be preceded and followed by independent clauses. A semicolon is used to emphasize the relatedness of the independent clauses.

Examples: I like to swim; Sally likes to go shopping.

I have a flight tomorrow morning; I need to go to bed early.

Semicolons can connect clauses joined by conjunctive adverbs such as *therefore*, *however*, and *in fact*.

Examples: I like to swim; however, Sally likes to go shopping.

I have a flight tomorrow morning; therefore, I need to go to bed early.

Drill 3 *Punctuate the following using colons and semicolons liberally.*
1. Pope Francis wrote out an extensive list groceries of all sorts rope an iPhone X and helium.
2. I haven't learned the basic rules of grammar nevertheless I believe that I will get a perfect score on the SAT.
3. I had an amazing time dancing singing and laughing.
4. I eat raw eggs which help me get stronger I want to become a body builder.
5. If there were an earthquake I would know what to do hide under my bed.
6. My favorite songs include "Stairway to Heaven" and "Hotel California" John's favorite songs include "Riptide" and "Gravity."

IV. Dashes —

Dashes can be used instead of commas to separate nonrestrictive elements. Dashes are more emphatic than commas.

Examples: William Shakespeare—who wrote my favorite play, *Hamlet*—is one of the most famous playwrights in history.

I am planning to attend the Ed Sheeran concert in TD Garden—where I met my husband, Tom.

Dashes can also replace colons that are followed by an explanation.

Examples: The cashier had a good reason to quit—his boss threatened to kill him after the cashier mischarged a customer.

The boy didn't understand calculus—he was only in 2nd grade.

Lastly, dashes can be used to create a dramatic pause in literary works.

Examples: Anyone who thinks he is the toughest guy in the room—clearly hasn't met me.

I worked all day to build a sand castle—only for it to be knocked over by waves during the rising tide.

Clauses and phrases between dashes don't count as part of the subject for subject-verb agreement.

Example: Harry—and his crazy ex-boyfriend—is at the party.

Drill 4 *Punctuate the following using dashes liberally*
1. I was told not to worry about my sister-in-law right before she started spray painting my car.
2. I asked for only two things peace and quiet.
3. After reviewing my boss' complaints all seventeen of them I realized I had a lot more work to do.
4. After seeing the party's aftermath a house that looked like it was falling apart and a lawn covered in puke and beer cans I decided never to host a party again.
5. I couldn't submit my final paper I was three minutes too late.
6. Alice Cooper told me that he has the heart of an eight-year old boy and he keeps it in a jar on his desk.

V. Quotation Marks ""

Short works like songs, TV episodes, and short poems are punctuated with quotation marks.

Example: "Heaven Knows I'm Miserable Now" is my favorite song.

Long works like novels, TV shows, and longer poems are italicized.

Example: *Breaking Bad* is my favorite TV show.

Use quotation marks for quotations that use the speakers' exact words.

Example: John F. Kennedy said, "Those who dare to fail miserably can achieve greatly."

Don't use quotation marks for something that is paraphrased.

Example: John F. Kennedy said daring to fail can lead to great success.

The first word in a complete sentence quotation is capitalized.

Example: Jill said, "The bathroom is out of service, but we have a porta potty in the backyard."

Quoted phrases and dependent clauses are only capitalized if they start a sentence.

Examples: Jill said the bathroom was "out of service" and that they had "a porta potty in the backyard."

"Bazinga" seemed like Jill's catchphrase.

Commas and periods go to the left of adjacent quotation marks.

Examples: "Why," John asked, "did you steal my pen?"

John said, "I needed my pen to take notes during class."

Semicolons, colons, and dashes go to the right of adjacent quotation marks.

Examples: My favorite song is "Don't Stop Believing"; I could listen to the song for hours.

I sang the first line of "Don't Stop Believing": "just a small town girl."

The pitcher said, "I will strike you out with my fastball"—as he held the baseball with a changeup grip.

Question marks and exclamation marks go to the left of adjacent quotation marks if the punctuation is part of the quotation.

Examples: "Why," John asked, "did you steal my pen?"

John said, "I needed my pen to take notes during class!"

Use single quotation marks to place a quotation inside another quotation.

Examples: Jack said, "'Don't Stop Believing' is my favorite song."

The witness said, "I heard John say, 'I hid the drugs in a secret compartment of my backpack.'"

Drill 5 *Determine if the sentence is grammatically correct. Correct all errors.*
1. I'm so mad that Jane said, "spaghetti tastes better than ramen"!
2. In Shakespeare's play "Macbeth", Macbeth becomes the king.
3. "How", Mary asked, "Did you manage to eat so quickly?"
4. "Don't Stop Believing" is about a girl from Detroit.
5. The boy said, "I would never steal from anyone;" I knew he was lying.
6. I can't believe that Daniel said, "My mother loves to listen to the song Stairway to Heaven"!

Punctuation Exercises

Determine if the sentence is grammatically correct. Correct all errors.

1. Yes, I am planning to see "Ozymandias," the widely acclaimed *Breaking Bad* episode.

2. John wanted to know why I woke up so early, "What were you doing up so early in the morning?"

3. Pastor Smith—who spent the previous night drinking at a wild college party—lectured us on the importance of religion.

4. After I saw the first-place prize, I redoubled my efforts to win my school's student of the year contest; even going so far as to cheat on my math test in order to get a higher score.

5. The manager always told the customers what they wanted to hear: delivering on her promises, however, was not her specialty.

6. My son told me about his most recent history class: "We had a substitute teacher who played a long tedious video about Eli Whitney."

7. George asked, "What did Karen mean when she said, 'I understand what you are going through'?"

8. John Smith—my friend from Atlanta, Georgia—is the kind of smart, caring person whom you would be lucky to meet.

9. The table tennis tournament will be held on: the first Friday of December.

10. I told my brother, "I don't know where your car keys are," however, I knew that I had left them at the house of my friend, Jake.

Answers

Punctuation Diagnostic

1. Not grammatically correct. The colon is not needed. Corrected: The tests this semester have been difficult, time-consuming, and unpredictable.
2. Grammatically correct
3. Not grammatically correct. *My* needs to be capitalized. Emily told me, "My favorite song is 'Stairway to Heaven.'"
4. Not grammatically correct. Friend needs to be followed by a period or semicolon. Corrected: John is my best friend; however, I don't always treat him as well as I should.
5. Not grammatically correct. A colon needs to be preceded by a complete sentence. The secret to making a big, tasty apple pie is to apply butter liberally.
6. Grammatically correct
7. Grammatically correct
8. Grammatically correct
9. Not grammatically correct. *Waiting for the bus to arrive* needs to be followed by a comma. Corrected: Waiting for the bus to arrive, I played video games on my phone—I didn't see the bus until it drove past me.
10. Not grammatically correct. Announcement should be followed by a colon. Corrected: The bus driver made an announcement: "This is the final stop."

Punctuation Drill 1

1. The success of *Breaking Bad*, a TV show produced by Vince Gilligan, demonstrates American audiences' fascination with drugs and violence.
2. Even after seven years, no one has found my wife's murderer. Moreover, there aren't any suspects.
3. The teacher whom I like more than any other is Linda Parker, who is patient and kind.
4. The family pet kitten, Paws, loved scratching the walls, which looked like they belonged on the set of a Wolverine movie.
5. Sarah and Rebecca went to the library to study for their upcoming biology test. I stayed home and watched *Footloose*.
6. In college, my girlfriend and I had practiced about twenty times for the play. Nevertheless, we both forgot our lines during the premiere.

Punctuation Drill 2

1. The large, fast kangaroo jumped over my head when I was asleep.
2. I went to the White House to meet President Trump, but he was too busy to speak to me.
3. My least favorite movies are *Clueless*, *The Godfather*, and *Ocean's 8*.
4. I took a long, deep breath, and then I shot the bright orange basketball into the hoop.
5. John picked up a small green wallet, but he didn't know whether to keep it, give it to the police, or ask someone nearby whether it belonged to him.
6. I want to learn how to swim without a life jacket, but I am too afraid of drowning or getting attacked by sharks.

Punctuation Drill 3

1. Pope Francis wrote out an extensive list: groceries of all sorts, rope, an iPhone X, and helium.
2. I haven't learned the basic rules of grammar; nevertheless, I believe that I will get a perfect score on the SAT.
3. I had an amazing time dancing, singing, and laughing.
4. I eat raw eggs, which help me get stronger; I want to become a body builder.
5. If there were an earthquake, I would know what to do: hide under my bed.
6. My favorite songs include "Stairway to Heaven" and "Hotel California"; John's favorite songs include "Riptide" and "Gravity."

Punctuation Drill 4

1. I was told not to worry about my sister-in-law—right before she started spray painting my car.
2. I asked for only two things—peace and quiet.
3. After reviewing my boss' complaints—all seventeen of them—I realized I had a lot more work to do.
4. After seeing the party's aftermath—a house that looked like it was falling apart and a lawn covered in puke and beer cans—I decided never to host a party again.
5. I couldn't submit my final paper—I was three minutes too late.
6. Alice Cooper told me that he has the heart of an eight-year-old boy—and he keeps it in a jar on his desk.

Punctuation Drill 5

1. Not grammatically correct. *Spaghetti* should be capitalized. Corrected: I'm so mad that Jane said, "Spaghetti tastes better than ramen"!
2. Not grammatically correct. The first *Macbeth* should be italicized. Corrected: In Shakespeare's play *Macbeth*, Macbeth becomes the king.
3. Not grammatically correct. The first comma should go before the quotation mark and *did* should not be capitalized. Corrected: "How," Mary asked, "did you manage to eat so quickly?"
4. Grammatically correct.
5. Not grammatically correct. The semicolon should go after the quotation mark. Corrected: The boy said, "I would never steal from anyone"; I knew he was lying.
6. Not grammatically correct. Stairway to Heaven should be punctuated with single quotation marks. Corrected: I can't believe that Daniel said, "My mother loves to listen to the song 'Stairway to Heaven'"!

Punctuation Exercises

1. Grammatically correct.
2. Not grammatically correct. The comma after *early* should be replaced with a colon. Corrected: John wanted to know why I woke up so early: "What were you doing up so early in the morning?"
3. Grammatically correct.
4. Not grammatically correct. The semicolon should be followed by a complete sentence. Corrected: After I saw the first-place prize, I redoubled my efforts to win my school's student of the year contest; I even went so far as to cheat on my math test in order to get a higher score.
5. Not grammatically correct. The colon should be followed with an explanation or illustration. Use a semicolon to separate two independent clauses. Corrected: The manager always told the customers what they wanted to hear; delivering on her promises, however, was not her specialty.
6. Not grammatically correct. *Long* and *tedious* should be separated by a comma. Corrected: My son told me about his most recent history class: "We had a substitute teacher who played a long, tedious video about Eli Whitney."
7. Grammatically correct.
8. Grammatically correct.
9. Not grammatically correct. The colon is not needed and should be removed. Corrected: The table tennis tournament will be held on the first Friday of December.
10. Not grammatically correct. There are two complete sentences that must be separated by a period or semicolon. Corrected: I told my brother, "I don't know where your car keys are." However, I knew that I had left them at the house of my friend, Jake.

The Comma with Restrictive and Nonrestrictive Elements

Diagnostic Test

Place commas where they are needed in these sentences. Some sentences will need none.

1. John Jacobs who is my brother borrowed my brand-new laptop which costs over one thousand dollars.

2. Chocolate cake with chocolate frosting is the dessert that I like best.

3. Uncle Bill sitting on the bench saw the murder that happened on Elm Street.

4. Donald George is the surgeon who is responsible for your Tommy John surgery which is a reconstruction of the ulnar collateral ligament (UCL) of the elbow.

5. William Shakespeare's play *Macbeth* is still being performed over 400 years after it was written.

6. *Harry Potter and the Sorcerer's Stone* a book by J. K. Rowling is about a boy named Harry Potter who finds out that he has magical powers.

7. Because of the earthquake in San Francisco, all planes scheduled to land at San Francisco International Airport one of the largest airports in the United States were rerouted to Oakland.

8. Drunk driving which is very dangerous is illegal in the United States.

9. Andover, Massachusetts settled in 1642 currently has a population of over 33,000 people all of whom clearly were not alive in 1642.

10. The man who stole my wallet is running towards the Charles River which is eighty miles long.

A. Restrictive Elements

A **restrictive element** is a clause or phrase that limits or specifies whatever it modifies. Therefore, restrictive elements are crucial to the intended meaning of the sentence and are not set off by commas.

- He has a dog *that follows him everywhere*. - *Dog that follows him everywhere* is more specific than *dog*. Therefore, *that follows him everywhere* is a clause that is a restrictive element.

- Jack Johnson is the man *singing from the stage*. - *The man singing from the stage* is more specific than *the man*. Therefore, *singing from the stage* is a phrase that is a restrictive element.

- My friend *Jake* will be at the concert. - Assuming that I have more than one friend, *my friend Jake* is more specific than *my friend*. Therefore, *Jake* is an appositive phrase that is a restrictive element.

B. Nonrestrictive Elements

A **nonrestrictive element** is a clause or phrase that doesn't limit or specify whatever it modifies. Therefore, nonrestrictive elements are not crucial to the intended meaning of the sentence. A nonrestrictive element is separated by commas from the rest of the sentence.

- Our team, *which has not won a game*, will not win any trophies. - *Our team* is as specific as *our team, which has not won a game*. Therefore, *which has not won a game* is a clause that is a nonrestrictive element.

- Jack Johnson, *singing from the stage*, attracted a large crowd. - *Jack Johnson* is as specific as *Jack Johnson, singing from the stage*. Therefore, *singing from the stage* is a phrase that is a nonrestrictive element.

- My best friend, *Jake*, will be at the concert. – Assuming that I have only one best friend, *My best friend* is as specific as *my best friend, Jake*. Therefore, *Jake* is an appositive phrase that is a nonrestrictive element.

C. One-of-a-kind people and things

An element is nonrestrictive whenever it modifies something that is one of a kind, because one-of-a-kind people and things can't be limited or specified any further.

- Aunt Pam, swimming in the pool, caught the football.
    - If I only have one Aunt Pam, then swimming in the pool is nonrestrictive
- I went to the grocery store to buy my favorite food, strawberries.
    - If I only have one favorite food, then strawberries is nonrestrictive
- The wedding's groom, George Smith, was nervous about getting married.
    - If there is only one groom at the wedding, then George Smith is nonrestrictive

D. That and Which

A modifying element that starts with the word "that" is restrictive, while a modifying element that starts with the word "which" is nonrestrictive.

- The movie that lasted four hours was really good.
- The movie, which lasted four hours, was really good.

The Comma with Restrictive Elements Exercises

Place commas where they are needed in these sentences. Some sentences will need none.

1. The place where I go to get my hair cut is offering a ten percent discount today.

2. The man with the dragon tattoo knows where to go to get a dragon egg that could hatch a green dragon.

3. My youngest child who is only eight years old told me that he wanted me to read him *Green Eggs and Ham* a book by Dr. Seuss.

4. My Economics 134 teacher Mr. House told the class that all students who got a perfect score on the most recent quiz could skip today's homework assignment.

5. George Orwell's book *1984* is even more relevant today, because today's technology which is only getting better can be used for mass surveillance.

6. George Cahill swimming in the pool drank alcohol which could have caused him to pass out and drown.

7. Trevor Story is the man who hit the farthest home run in today's game which lasted over four hours.

8. The success of *Breaking Bad* a TV show produced by Vince Gilligan demonstrates American audiences' fascination with drugs and violence.

9. The teacher whom I like more than any other is Linda Parker who is patient and kind.

10. The family pet kitten Paws loved scratching the walls which looked like they belonged on the set of a Wolverine movie.

11. The girl in my geometry class who got the highest score on the test told me that she studied for eight hours which was twice as long as I had studied.

12. During my first visit to the restaurant, my waiter who looked like he was still in middle school recommended that I order a bacon cheeseburger with fries.

13. My wife Judy and I loved our trip to the spa that was only a ten-minute drive from our house.

14. During the principal's speech, he announced that any student who gets caught smoking marijuana will be expelled and that his or her parents will not receive any reimbursement of tuition which is over $40,000 per year.

15. Edgar Allen Poe born in 1809 is most remembered for his poem "The Raven".

16. The store employee who gave me a menacing look could tell that I was a man who was up to no good.

17. In the movie *National Treasure* starring Nicolas Cage, the Declaration of Independence which was written in 1776 contains a coded map to the location of buried treasure that hasn't been seen for centuries.

18. My favorite movie *The Shawshank Redemption* is about an innocent man who gets arrested for murder.

19. The most difficult part of a life that lasts over one hundred years is living without family members and friends whom you love dearly.

20. I am one of the few applicants who made it to the second round of interviews for the job that I want more than anything in the world.

Answers

The Comma with Restrictive Element Diagnostic

1. John Jacobs, who is my brother, borrowed my brand-new laptop, which costs over one thousand dollars.

2. Chocolate cake with chocolate frosting is the food that I like best.

3. Uncle Bill, sitting on the bench, saw the murder that happened on Elm Street.

4. Donald George is the surgeon who is responsible for your Tommy John surgery, which is a reconstruction of the ulnar collateral ligament (UCL) of the elbow.

5. William Shakespeare's play *Macbeth* is still being performed over 400 years after it was written.

6. *Harry Potter and the Sorcerer's Stone*, a book by J. K. Rowling, is about a boy named Harry Potter, who finds out that he has magical powers.

7. Because of the earthquake in San Francisco, all planes scheduled to land at San Francisco International Airport, one of the largest airports in the United States, were rerouted to Oakland.

8. Drunk driving, which is very dangerous, is illegal in the United States.

9. Andover, Massachusetts, settled in 1642, currently has a population of over 33,000 people, all of whom clearly were not alive in 1642.

10. The man who stole my wallet is running towards the Charles River, which is eighty miles long.

The Comma with Restrictive Element Exercises

1. The place where I go to get my hair cut is offering a ten percent discount today.

2. The man with the dragon tattoo knows where to go to get a dragon egg that could hatch a green dragon.

3. My youngest child, who is only eight years old, told me that he wanted me to read him *Green Eggs and Ham*, a book by Dr. Seuss.

4. My Economics 134 teacher, Mr. House, told the class that all students who got a perfect score on the most recent quiz could skip today's homework assignment.

5. George Orwell's book *1984* is even more relevant today, because today's technology, which is only getting better, can be used for mass surveillance.

6. George Cahill, swimming in the pool, drank alcohol, which could have caused him to pass out and drown.

7. Trevor Story is the man who hit the farthest home run in today's game, which lasted over four hours.

8. The success of *Breaking Bad*, a TV show produced by Vince Gilligan, demonstrates American audiences' fascination with drugs and violence.

9. The teacher whom I like more than any other is Linda Parker, who is patient and kind.

10. The family pet kitten, Paws, loved scratching the walls, which looked like they belonged on the set of a Wolverine movie.

11. The girl in my geometry class who got the highest score on the test told me that she studied for eight hours, which was twice as long as I had studied.

12. During my first visit to the restaurant, my waiter, who looked like he was still in middle school, recommended that I order a bacon cheeseburger with fries.

13. My wife, Judy, and I loved our trip to the spa that was only a ten-minute drive from our house.

14. During the principal's speech, he announced that any student who gets caught smoking marijuana will be expelled and that his or her parents will not receive any reimbursement of tuition, which is over $40,000 per year.

15. Edgar Allen Poe, born in 1809, is most remembered for his poem "The Raven".

16. The store employee who gave me a menacing look could tell that I was a man who was up to no good.

17. In the movie *National Treasure*, starring Nicolas Cage, the Declaration of Independence, which was written in 1776, contains a coded map to the location of buried treasure that hasn't been seen for centuries.

18. My favorite movie, *The Shawshank Redemption*, is about an innocent man who gets arrested for murder.

19. The most difficult part of a life that lasts over one hundred years is living without family members and friends whom you love dearly.

20. I am one of the few applicants who made it to the second round of interviews for the job that I want more than anything in the world.

Run-on Sentences

Diagnostic Test

Repair each sentence that is a run-on sentence or fragment.

1. This year my birthday falls on a Saturday, we shall have a party that lasts twenty-four hours.

2. I looked everywhere for my wallet, however I never found it.

3. Please lend me your car after you get home from work, I need to pick up my prescription, but my car is still in the shop.

4. After waiting an hour for my boyfriend to arrive, I decided to eat without him, because I was very hungry.

5. "I see a mouse right next to the lamp," he shrieked, "I hope it stays away from me."

6. My dog is very friendly towards everyone in my family, however, she is very vicious towards everyone else.

7. I decided to surprise my wife by buying a trip to the Bahamas, but when I told her my plan she told me that she didn't want to go, because she had to complete a big project at work.

8. I can't believe my brother decided to marry Jessica, she was arrested three different times for drug possession.

9. I saw a man with a gun charging towards me, overcome by fear, I just stood there until he was right in front of me.

10. The clumsy boy forgot to do his homework, consequently, he told the teacher that he left his homework at home.

Run-on Sentences

Recall that an independent clause is a clause that makes sense on its own. Two or more independent clauses joined together without a conjunction, period, semi-colon, or colon make a grammatical error called a **run-on** sentence.

I. Commas

A comma can't be used to separate independent clauses even when the clauses are related.

Examples: Run-on: I play hockey, my sister plays volleyball.
Fixed: I play hockey. My sister plays volleyball.

| I | play | hockey |

| sister | plays | volleyball |
        \my

Run-on: The homework assignment is difficult, you should start immediately.
Fixed: The homework assignment is difficult. You should start immediately.

Run-on: I scored twenty points, you scored only eight points.
Fixed: I scored twenty points. You scored only eight points.

Run-on: I decided to go to medical school, I want to become a doctor.
Fixed: I decided to go to medical school. I want to become a doctor.

II. Conjunctions

Independent clauses need to be connected by the proper conjunctions.

Use ***coordinating conjunctions*** to combine equally important sentence elements. The major coordinating conjunctions are: *for*, *and*, *not*, *but*, *or*, *yet*, and *so*.

Examples: I went to the store to buy some milk, *but* I ended up also buying some ice cream.

I went to the beach *and* Sally went shopping.

Our favorite roller coaster was shut down, *yet* we had a great time.

Use ***subordinating conjunctions*** to introduce a clause of lesser importance. Consider the following examples:

Examples: *If* I had known how to swim, I would have jumped into the pool and saved the drowning girl. (*if* is the subordinating conjunction and *if I had known how to swim* is the subordinate clause)

I will attend the party *unless* you tell me not to come. (*unless* is the subordinating conjunction and *unless you tell me not to come* is the subordinate clause)

Once I get my driver's license, I will drive to Ohio to visit my grandmother. (*once* is the subordinating conjunction and *once I get my driver's license* is the subordinate clause)

Common subordinating conjunctions include:

after	that	unless
although	once	until
as	provided	when
because	that	whenever
before	rather than	where
even if	since	whereas
even	so that	wherever
though	than	while
if	that	why
in order	though	

Use ***correlative conjunctions***, which are tag-team conjunctions, to link two of the same type of sentence element.

Examples: *If* you understand this lesson, *then* you will do well on the exercises.

Either I am hallucinating *or* you just stole candy from the convenience store.

I would *rather* visit my grandmother *than* go to your birthday party.

The more common correlative conjunctions include:

As ... as	Just as ... so	Such ... as
Both ... and	Neither ... nor	Such ... that
Between ... and	Not only ... but also	So ... that
Either ... or	No sooner ... than	What with ... and
From ... to	Not ... but	Whether ... or
Hardly ... when	Rather ... than	
If ... then	Scarcely ... when	

In summary, coordinating conjunctions combine equally important sentence elements, subordinating conjunctions introduce nonessential clauses, and correlative conjunctions work in pairs to create a relationship between sentence elements.

A. Transitional Elements aren't Conjunctions

Some words that look like conjunctions are not and should not be used as conjunctions. For example, the following transitional elements should not be used as conjunctions: consequently, therefore, however, nevertheless, in fact, and moreover.

Examples: Run-on: Jake skipped class yesterday, consequently he is behind on his schoolwork.
Fixed: Jake skipped class yesterday. Consequently, he is behind on his schoolwork.
Fixed: Jake skipped class yesterday, and so he is behind on his schoolwork.

Run-on: I don't think we will win, nevertheless I will try my best.
Fixed: I don't think we will win. Nevertheless, I will try my best.
Fixed: I don't think we will win, but I will try my best.

Drill 1 *Repair each sentence that is a run-on sentence or fragment.*
1. You don't need to answer all of the questions, answer as many as you can in the time allotted.
2. Of course I knew that the answer was eight, in fact I wrote down eight on my answer sheet.
3. No sooner did I arrive at the station than the bus came.
4. I need to do my homework, however I can do it after the party.
5. John and Sarah went to the football game last night, I stayed home to finish my college applications.
6. A man who dropped his wallet walked out of the train station, therefore he never saw his wallet again.

B. Fixing Run-ons with Subordinate Clauses

One way to fix a run-on sentence is by using subordinating conjunctions to convert all but one of the independent clauses into subordinate clauses.

Run-on: I will study all night for the test, I want a good grade.
Fixed: I will study all night for the test, because I want a good grade.

Run-on : All of the libraries at our school have metal detectors, this makes it more difficult to sneak a gun into our libraries.
Fixed: All of the libraries at our school have metal detectors, which make it more difficult to sneak a gun into our libraries.

C. Quotations

Examples: "Harry is marrying Sally," he shouted.
John asked, "When is Harry marrying Sally?"

The above sentences are not run-ons because the quotations act as direct objects to *he shouted* and *John asked*.

Whenever a complete sentence introduces a quotation, use a colon to avoid a run-on sentence.

Example: Run-on: J. K. Rowling opens the Harry Potter series by introducing the Dursleys, "Mr. and Mrs. Dursley, of number four, Privet Drive, were proud to say that they were perfectly normal, thank you very much."
Fixed: J. K. Rowling opens the Harry Potter series by introducing the Dursleys: "Mr. and Mrs. Dursley, of number four, Privet Drive, were proud to say that they were perfectly normal, thank you very much."

Whenever a quotation is split into two complete sentences, place a period after whatever introduces the quotations.

Example: Run-on: "I want to meet your brother," he said, "I was told that he has a job opportunity for me."
Fixed: "I want to meet your brother," he said. "I was told that he has a job opportunity for me."

D. Multiple Clauses or Phrases

A sentence with multiple clauses or phrases is a run-on if the sentence can be divided into two complete sentences. The best places to try dividing a sentence are in between clauses and phrases.

Examples: Although this sentence has three clauses, and the clauses are different, this is not a run-on sentence.

Run-on: The man thought his life passed by quickly even though he loved every minute of it, nevertheless he already was eighty years old.
Fixed: The man thought his life passed by quickly even though he loved every minute of it. Nevertheless, he already was eighty years old.

Run-on: The Corvette crashed into a wall, flying out of his seat, the driver smacked into the windshield.
Fixed: The Corvette crashed into a wall. Flying out of his seat, the driver smacked into the windshield.

Drill 2 *Repair each sentence that is a run-on sentence or fragment.*

1. I will continue learning while I wait for my SAT result, I am anxious about my result.

2. "I try to make all of my free throws," he said, "The problem is that I don't have enough practice."

3. In his play *The Tempest*, William Shakespeare suggests that some people might be evil: "Hell is empty and all the devils are here."

4. Furthermore, I will be waiting for you, and I will be ready to give you your car keys back even though I never got to try driving your car.

5. "What happened here? It looks like a wild bear attacked this room," whispered the police officer.

6. The team that wins the championship will get commemorative diamond rings worth tens of thousands of dollars, it is a lot of money.

Run-on Sentences Exercises

Repair each sentence that is a run-on sentence or fragment.

1. "I am sorry that I didn't call you," he said, "I would have called you if I knew that you needed my help."

2. The hurricane turned books and lamps into dangerous projectiles, hiding in the closet, Harry managed to survive the ordeal.

3. Although I didn't hear or see anyone, and my roommate told me that he wouldn't come home until midnight, I was convinced that he was hiding somewhere in the apartment.

4. Everyone knew that Mary was lying, in fact someone in the class even told the teacher that Mary's story didn't add up.

5. While watching the tennis ball coming towards me, I could tell that the ball probably would bounce to the left, because I saw the ball's sidespin.

6. "I did not borrow your laptop," I insisted, "Why would I even need it?

7. Sarah and Rebecca went to the library to study for their upcoming biology test, I stayed home and watched *Footloose*.

8. After hours of running, I saw the finish line, at last I could complete the marathon.

9. No one has found my wife's murderer, moreover there aren't any suspects.

10. My girlfriend and I had practiced about twenty times for the play, nevertheless we both forgot our lines during the premiere.

Answers

Diagnostic

1. This year my birthday falls on a Saturday. We shall have a party that lasts twenty-four hours.
2. I looked everywhere for my wallet, but I never found it.
3. Please lend me your car after you get home from work. I need to pick up my prescription, but my car is still in the shop.
4. N/A
5. "I see a mouse right next to the lamp," he shrieked. "I hope it stays away from me."
6. My dog is very friendly towards everyone in my family, but very vicious towards everyone else.
7. N/A
8. I can't believe my brother decided to marry Jessica. She was arrested three different times for drug possession.
9. I saw a man with a gun charging towards me. Overcome by fear, I just stood there until he was right in front of me.
10. The clumsy boy forgot to do his homework. Consequently, he told the teacher that he left his homework at home.

Drill 1

1. You don't need to answer all of the questions. Answer as many as you can in the time allotted.
2. Of course I knew that the answer was eight. In fact, I wrote down eight on my answer sheet.
3. N/A
4. I need to do my homework. However, I can do it after the party.
5. John and Sarah went to the football game last night. I stayed home to finish my college applications.
6. A man who dropped his wallet walked out of the train station and never saw his wallet again.

Drill 2

1. I will continue learning while I wait for my SAT result. I am anxious about my result.
2. "I try to make all of my free throws," he said. "The problem is that I don't have enough practice."
3. N/A
4. N/A
5. N/A
6. The team that wins the championship will get commemorative diamond rings worth tens of thousands of dollars, which is a lot of money.

Exercises

1. "I am sorry that I didn't call you," he said. "I would have called you if I knew that you needed my help."
2. The hurricane turned books and lamps into dangerous projectiles. Hiding in the closet, Harry managed to survive the ordeal.
3. N/A
4. Everyone knew that Mary was lying. In fact, someone in the class even told the teacher that Mary's story didn't add up.
5. N/A
6. "I did not borrow your laptop," I insisted. "Why would I even need it?
7. While Sarah and Rebecca went to the library to study for their upcoming biology test, I stayed home and watched *Footloose*.
8. After hours of running, I saw the finish line. At last I could complete the marathon.
9. No one has found my wife's murderer. Moreover, there aren't any suspects.
10. My girlfriend and I had practiced about twenty times for the play. Nevertheless we both forgot our lines during the premiere.

Diction

Diagnostic Test

Select the word that makes the most sense.

1. In order to find out where his daughter was being held captive, Liam Neeson tried to (A. elicit B. illicit) a response from the criminal.
2. Many hotels offer (A. complimentary B. complementary) breakfast.
3. I wish to have a positive (A. affect B. effect) on my younger brother.
4. I need to (A. rise B. raise) early in the morning in order to get to work on time.
5. The cat has (A. laid B. lain) on the bed for hours.
6. The mental patient suffered from (A. allusions B. delusions C. illusions).
7. The bear that killed my father is (A. amoral B. immoral).
8. Lebron James is an (A. eminent B. imminent) athlete.
9. I would rather fight one hundred duck-sized horses (A. than B. then) fight a horse-sized duck.
10. I ran (A. passed B. past) a teacher in the hallway.
11. Running for hours is (A. exhaustive B. exhausting).
12. I ran (A. farther B. further) than I did yesterday.
13. Fictional characters are (A. imaginary B. imaginative).
14. I was arrested for possession of an (A. elicit B. illicit) substance.
15. The woman told me to keep our affair (A. discreet B. discrete) because she didn't want her husband to find out.
16. I hope that parking fines are eliminated (A. altogether B. all together).
17. Some people like him, but even more people dislike him—no one is (A. ambivalent B. ambiguous) about him.
18. The restaurant wants to hire a (A. complacent B. complaisant) hostess to make its customers feel better.
19. My mentor will (A. council B. counsel) me tonight.
20. I don't trust the woman sitting (A. beside B. besides) me.

Diction

"What can you add to this company?"

 "The skill set of your workers in conjecture with mine would be a great mix. My skills would be complimentary to theirs. Moreover, my skills will raise to any challenge."

It is important to choose the right words. For example, there is a big difference between an *imaginary* person and an *imaginative* person. An *imaginary* person only exists in the imagination, but an *imaginative* person is a creative person.

I. Affect and Effect

Affect is a verb meaning to make a difference to.

Examples: The wind *affected* my ability to accurately throw a ball.

The money that I donated to the senator *affected* his policies.

Effect can be a noun meaning a difference that is caused by someone or something.

Examples: The wind had an *effect* on my ability to accurately throw a ball.

The senator claims that my donations didn't have an *effect* on his policies.

Effect can also be a verb meaning to bring about.

Examples: For the good of the school, the principal *effected* a policy of zero tolerance to smoking. (the principal created the policy)

The senator said that after years of a stalling economy, the bill would *effect* an economic boom. (meaning cause an economic boom and not just change it)

Drill 1 *Select the word that makes the most sense.*
1. The mouse was (A. affected B. effected) by the chemicals.
2. One (A. affect B. effect) of the bill will be a decreased murder rate.

3. Seeing his father smoke marijuana (A. affected B. effected) the boy's opinion of his father.
4. I hope to (A. affect B. effect) your use of affect and effect.
5. The lack of sunlight had a strong (A. affect B. effect) on the prisoner's psyche.
6. The researcher wants to (A. affect B. effect) a cure for cancer because there isn't a cure and his mother is dying of cancer.

II. Allusion, Delusion, and Illusion

Allusion is a noun meaning a reference to or a mention of.

Examples: The ending line "to be or not to be" was an *allusion* to Shakespeare.

Taylor Swift wrote a new song that contains an *allusion* to one of her ex-boyfriends.

Delusion is a noun meaning a firmly implanted misconception that disagrees with conventional wisdom.

Examples: Kyrie Irving has a *delusion* that the Earth is flat.

The mental hospital patient suffers from the *delusion* that everyone else is a robot.

Illusion is a noun meaning a thing that is or is likely to be wrongly perceived.

Examples: The magician uses optical *illusions* in his magic tricks.

When looking at the *illusion*, some people think that the shorter line is longer than the longer line.

Drill 2 *Select the word that makes the most sense.*
1. The conspiracy theorist told me that his belief that the moon landing was faked is not (A. an allusion B. a delusion C. an illusion).
2. I thought that I saw a bird, but it turned out to be (A. an allusion B. a delusion C. an illusion).
3. Literary writers often use (A. allusions B. delusions C. illusions) to improve their writing.

III. Complement and Compliment

Complement can be a noun meaning a thing that makes a group complete.

Examples: Spaghetti is a perfect *complement* to meatballs.

Yin is the *complement* of yang.

Complement can also be a verb meaning to add to something in a way that enhances it.

Examples: The spaghetti *complements* the meatballs.

Yin *complements* yang.

Compliment can be a noun meaning a polite expression or praise.

Examples: In an effort to increase his tip, the waiter gave me a *compliment.*

The best *compliment* that you've given me occurred when you called me smart.

Compliment can also be a verb meaning to give someone a compliment (polite expression or praise).

Examples: In an effort to increase his tip, the waiter *complimented* me.

I *complimented* my friend on his honesty.

IV. Complementary and Complimentary

Complementary is an adjective meaning combining in such a way as to enhance.

Examples: Spaghetti and meatballs are *complementary*.

The drummer and the guitarist played *complementary* parts.

Complimentary is an adjective that can mean expressing a compliment.

Examples: The waiter was *complimentary*.

I use *complimentary* language so that people will enjoy talking to me.

Complimentary is an adjective that can also mean free of charge.

Examples: The hotel breakfast was *complimentary*.

After my interview, I received a *complimentary* notebook that had the company's logo on the front cover.

Drill 3 *Select the word that makes the most sense.*
1. I didn't need to pay for the lunch because it was (A. complementary B. complimentary).
2. I think that tie (A. complements B. compliments) your suit.

3. Management instructed the cashiers to be more (A. complementary B. complimentary) towards customers.
4. I love receiving (A. complements B. compliments) because they increase my self-esteem.
5. I think that brownies and ice cream are (A. complementary B. complimentary).

V. Amount vs. Number and Fewer vs. Less

Number and fewer are used for countable nouns.

Examples: The boy could only carry two or fewer grocery bags at one time.

I saw a number of my classmates performing at the school play.

The chef struggled to make the dish because he had fewer ingredients than he was accustomed to.

Amount and less are used for uncountable nouns.

Examples: It rained less than I expected.

I was impressed by the amount of exuberance in the room.

I picked up less food at the grocery store than I normally do.

For measurements, less is used unless the writer wants to enumerate the measurement.

Examples: I ran less than five miles.

You must respond in fewer than ten days to be considered (nine days and twenty-three hours won't be soon enough)

Drill 4 *Select the word that makes the most sense.*
1. The plaintiff would not accept a plea bargain for (A. fewer B. less) than $5,000.
2. I was shocked by the large (A. amount B. number) of bugs in our attic.
3. I wish that there were (A. fewer B. less) sand at my local beach.
4. I drink (A. fewer B. less) cups of coffee than she does.
5. A large (A. amount B. number) of water spilled on the floor.
6. I prefer websites that have (A. fewer B. less) advertisements.

VI. Lay and Lie

	Now	Yesterday	Over Time
to recline	I lie down	I lay down	I have lain down
to place	I lay the book on the table	I laid the book on the table	I have laid the book on the table

In present tense, the difference between **lay** and **lie** is that *lay* is a transitive verb (which requires a direct object) and *lie* is an intransitive verb (no direct object). In other words, people *lay* something down and *lie* down by themselves.

Examples: He *lays* the book on the table.

   He *lies* down on the sofa.

The past tense of *lie* is *lay*. The past tense of *lay* is *laid*.

Examples: He *laid* the book on the table.

   He *lay* down on the sofa.

The past participle of *lie* is *lain*. The past participle of *lay* is *laid*.

Examples: He has *laid* the book on the table.

   He has *lain* down on the sofa for hours.

Drill 5 *Select the word that makes the most sense.*
1. Tell Sally to (A. lay B. lie) down.
2. Last night, I (A. laid B. lay C. lied) the book on the table.
3. Yesterday, I (A. laid B. lay C. lied) down on the grass.
4. The book has (A. laid B. lain) on the table for days.
5. The teacher (A. laid B. lay C. lied) the apple on the table.
6. I have (A. laid B. lain) the lamp on the table.

VII. Past and Passed

Past and ***passed*** can be confused especially when describing movement. *Passed* is never used when describing time.

Examples: I *passed* all of my exams.

   I *passed* other students in the hallway.

   John *passed* the ball to Meghan.

   The catcher was charged with a *passed* ball.

Passed can be the past tense or past participle (act as adjectives) of the verb *to pass*. To pass means to go forward, proceed, or depart.

When referring to movement, *past* can be a preposition or adverb. As a preposition, *past* means to or on the further side of.

Example: The bathroom is *past* the chandelier.

   I drove *past* the bank.

As an adverb, *past* means passing from one side of something to the other.

Example: The train went *past*.

   I saw a shark swimming *past*.

Determining the part of speech will help with deciding between passed and past. Assuming the word describes movement, choose *passed* for verbs and adjectives and choose *past* for prepositions and adverbs.

Drill 6 *Select the word that makes the most sense.*
1. The ball went (A. passed B. past) my first base and hit a spectator.
2. I (A. passed B. past) six different clocks in the hallway.
3. There is a bathroom (A. passed B. past) the cafeteria.
4. The job candidate (A. passed B. past) all of my expectations.

VIII. Rise and Raise

	Now	Yesterday	Over Time
move up	I rise	I rose	I have risen
lift something up	I raise	I raised	I have raised

Examples: I *raised* my hand. (The direct object, *my hand*, was raised)

The temperature will *rise* in the afternoon. (The subject, *temperature*, rose)

I believe that many helping hands can *raise* the boat. (The direct object, *the boat*, was raised)

I don't expect my test score to *rise* after it gets re-graded. (The subject, *test score*, rose)

Rise and raise are very similar. They both mean to move to a higher position. The difference is that **raise** is a transitive verb and the direct object moves to a higher position. On the other hand, **rise** is an intransitive verb and the subject of the verb moves to a higher position.

Drill 7 *Select the word that makes the most sense.*
1. The balloon (A. rose B. raised) off the ground.
2. The wind (A. rose B. raised) my umbrella.
3. The unemployment rate (A. rose B. raised) this year because many companies went out of business.
4. If you have your hand on the button, you can (A. rise B. raise) your hand.

IX. There, Their, and They're

There can be an adverb meaning in, at, or to that place or position or there can be used to call attention to something. There can also be used as an expletive to focus attention on something.

Examples: If my memory serves me correctly, a murder happened over *there*. (adjective)

There are many ways to catch fish. (expletive)

Their is a possessive pronoun meaning belonging to the people previously mentioned.

Examples: I gave the students *their* cell phones back.

The teachers tried *their* best.

They're is a contraction for they are.

Examples: *They're* getting married.

I told my brothers that *they're* not as smart as I am.

Drill 8 *Select the word that makes the most sense.*
1. Two students forgot to bring (A. there B. their C. they're) notebooks.
2. The car accident happened over (A. there B. their C. they're).
3. I have never met your brothers, but I heard that (A. there B. their C. they're) handsome.

X. Swam and Swum

The past tense of swim can either be swam or swum. Use swum when it is preceded by a helping verb. Otherwise, use swam.

Examples: I *swam* to the island.

I have *swum* to the island.

Drill 9 *Select the word that makes the most sense.*
1. Have you (A. swam B. swum) in your pool yet?
2. I have (A. swam B. swum) in my pool.
3. I (A. swam B. swum) over two miles today.

XI. Other Commonly Confused Words

adverse means harmful; unfavorable   **averse** means opposed to

aggravate means make something negative even worse or more serious   **annoy** means to irritate someone

already means before or by the time in question   **all ready** means to be entirely prepared

altar means table for religious ceremony   **alter** means to change

altogether means completely   **all together** means all in one place or time

a lot means a large number of something   **allot** means to give out something to someone as a share or task

ambivalent means mixed feelings about something   **ambiguous** means having a double meaning

amoral means lacking a moral sense   **immoral** means unethical or wrongful

208

ascent means movement up

assent means agreement or to agree

bare means not clothed or covered

bear means to carry, support, endure, give birth to, or turn in a specific direction

bated means in great suspense

baited means deliberately annoy or taunt or it means to prepare a hook or trap with bait to entice animals

beside means next to something

besides means in addition to something

breath means air that goes into and out of lungs

breathe means to draw air into and expel it from the lungs

canvas means a strong cloth

canvass means to ask people their opinions

capital means money or most important city

capitol means building for legislature

complacent means feeling you barely need to try

complaisant means willing to please others

conscience means inner voice or feeling acting as a moral compass

conscious means aware of and responding to one's surroundings

council means an elected group of people

counsel means to give advice

councilor means a member of a council

counselor means a trained adviser

dessert means a sweet food

desert means a hot, dry area

discover means to find or locate something

invent means to create or design

discreet means secretive

discrete means separate and distinct

disinterested means impartial

uninterested means not interested

elicit means to evoke or draw out an answer from someone in reaction to one's own actions

illicit means forbidden by rules or custom

eminent means respected

imminent means about to happen

empathy means the ability to understand another

sympathy means feelings of pity

everyday means commonplace

every day means each day

every one means each or each individual item or person

everyone means all the people in a group

exhaustive means comprehensive

exhausting means tiring

explicit means stated clearly and in detail with no room for confusion or doubt

implicit means implied though not plainly expressed

farther means greater physical distance

further means greater metaphorical distance

flaunt means to ostentatiously display something

flout means openly disregard

hanged means killed by hanging

hung means suspended

hoard means stockpile

horde means a large group of people

imaginary means fictional or nonexistent

imaginative means creative or visionary

imply means to suggest without expressly stating

infer means to deduce from evidence and reasoning rather than from explicit statements

ingenious means really clever

ingenuous means innocent and unsuspecting

its means belongs to

it's means it is

later means more late than something

latter means near the end of something

miner means a mine worker

minor means not important

moral means rights and wrongs

morale means confidence, enthusiasm, and discipline

personal means relating to a particular person

personnel means people employed in an organization

premier means first in position, time, rank, or importance

premiere means the first performance, or it means to give the first performance of

prescribe means to advise or authorize the use of a rule or treatment

proscribe means to forbid

principal means the first or most important or the first or most important person or money

principle means a basic rule

rational means reasonable

rationale means the reason

respectfully means showing respect

respectively means in the same order

stationary means not moving

stationery means office supplies

than is used for comparisons

then is used for time

whose means which person

who's means who is

XII. Adjectives and Adverbs

Choosing the correct adjective or adverb is an issue relating to diction.

Adjectives and **adverbs** are two of the eight parts of speech in English. Adjectives are different from adverbs that modify verbs, adjectives, or other verbs, but are often used incorrectly in each other's place.

A. An adjective is a word that modifies a noun or pronoun. Adjectives answer "what kind?" or "which?" or "how many?"

- The king wore a *heavy golden* crown.
- The *smartest* pupil in the room is Andy.
- There are *seven* trees in my yard.

B. An adverb describes a verb, adjective or other adverbs. Adverbs answer "how?" or "when?" or "where?" or "why?" or "to what extent?"

- The politician spoke *persuasively*.
- *Unfortunately*, my friend did not gain admission to her safety school.

Drill 10 *Replace the incorrect words or mark the sentence correct if it is correct.*

1. The football player was not wearing his helmet proper and the looseness of its fit caused it to fall off during a strenuous game exposing the young athlete's cranium to a sudden concussion.

2. The tiramisu at Bertucci's tastes sweetly but ends the meal just right after the antipasto, the spaghetti a la Bolognese and the glass of Chianti.

3. When the key did not slide silent into the keyhole, the proctor in charge of the dormitory rushed to the door to apprehend the student, who in returning to the dormitory beyond the curfew hour could not preclude his entry from detection.

4. When the roads are hazardous at the beginning of a rainstorm as the drops of precipitation mix with the oily tar of the road's surface, drivers traveling over the sudden slickness of the surface are advised to drive slow.

5. When your writing assignment is done correct then you feel that you have accomplished something important and that you can therefore, after submitting your work to your teacher, get on with your life.

6. Organic farmers have discovered that by gathering seeds from the very plants they cultivate, they no longer need to purchase seeds, and in taking advantage of what they already have accumulated, can offer the public at a significant profit their inexpensive grown produce.

7. The pollsters who work for politicians running for office need to take into account the constantly changing voter preferences, which are varied and capricious day to day.

8. Though the diligent student persevered in her studies to prepare herself for the SAT, once she came to the last section, which was a long and challenging passage to read, she had to leave five answers blank because she could not get through the material quick enough to finish the section on time.

9. He handles the ball good; in the last game after the coach had noticed his quick passes and clever moves, the coach made him the point guard of the team for the rest of the season.

10. The omelet tastes nutty because within its texture lies grated bits of Swiss cheese.

Diction Exercises

Select the word that makes the most sense.

1. The quality of your education (A. affects B. effects) your reading comprehension.
2. The best way to (A. raise B. rise) your test scores is to study more often.
3. The only part that I've paid is the (A. principal B. principle).
4. Instructions are easier to understand when they are (A. explicit B. implicit).
5. I suspect that the (A. eminent B. imminent) winter will be warmer than last year.
6. After dinner, I will eat (A. dessert B. desert).
7. I (A. passed B. past) my math teacher in the hallway.
8. My brother was (A. complimentary B. complementary) before asking for a favor.
9. My sons forgot (A. there B. their C. they're) homework.
10. I haven't read the (A. later B. latter) part of the book.
11. People who are sleeping are not (A. conscience B. conscious).
12. The teacher was not (A. adverse B. averse) to using corporal punishment.
13. The office secretary is going to Staples to get more (A. stationary B. stationery).
14. The politician told her assistant to (A. canvas B. canvass) the neighborhood.
15. The doctor (A. prescribed B. proscribed) me medicine for my cold.
16. I (A. hanged B. hung) stockings next to the Christmas tree.
17. I could not (A. bare B. bear) telling my brother that his girlfriend died in a car crash.
18. I hope to (A. altar B. alter) your opinion.
19. Have you ever (A. swam B. swum) at the beach?
20. After school I (A. laid B. lied) down on my bed to get some rest.
21. The boy was (A. already B. all ready) to start the day.
22. I am so (A. ingenious B. ingenuous) that I don't know how babies are made.
23. I watched the (A. ascent B. assent) of the rocket.
24. My dad taught me not to worry about (A. miner B. minor) details.
25. The child (A. bated B. baited) his younger sister into hitting him.
26. The sleeping man was (A. disinterested B. uninterested) in the game and only went because his brother was playing.
27. I brush my teeth (A. everyday B. every day).

28. My shoes (A. complement B. compliment) my suit.

29. Amy and Brian are five and ten years old, (A. respectfully B. respectively).

30. My (A. rational B. rationale) for choosing UC Berkeley is its lower tuition.

31. The (A. hoard B. horde) of townspeople is approaching my house.

32. Tell my brother to (A. lay B. lie) down.

33. I asked my parents to (A. allot B. a lot) me more time on the computer.

34. I went with my father to work at the (A. capital B. capitol) building.

35. Please return the book back to (A. its B. it's) place in the cabinet.

36. The man liked to stare at (A. allusions B. delusions C. illusions) because they allowed him to see what wasn't there.

37. (A. Whose B. Who's) responsible for the investigation?

38. It is (A. amoral B. immoral) to kill someone.

39. The reading passage didn't state who killed the maid, but it (A. implied B. inferred) who killed her.

40. The mischievous student liked to (A. flaunt B. flout) the rules.

41. I decided to go to the movie (A. premier B. premiere).

42. The pirate fought and plundered until his last (A. breathe B. breath).

43. All Chipotle (A. personal B. personnel) spent the day learning about food safety.

44. I tried to raise the (A. morale B. moral) of the boy who had his head down.

45. Christopher Columbus is well renowned for (A. discovering B. inventing) the Americas.

46. The swamp monster had a heightened (A. empathy B. sympathy) for human emotions.

47. The employee asked the boss to have (A. fewer B. less) meetings.

48. I asked the school guidance (A. councilor B. counselor) for a college recommendation.

49. (A. Every one B. Everyone) of the brothers was at the party.

50. I told the waitress to put a small (A. amount B. number) of ice cubes in my water.

Answers

Diagnostic

1. A. elicit
2. A. complimentary
3. B. effect
4. A. rise
5. B. lain
6. B. delusions
7. A. amoral
8. A. eminent
9. A. than
10. B. past
11. B. exhausting
12. A. farther
13. A. imaginary
14. B. illicit
15. A. discreet
16. A. altogether
17. A. ambivalent
18. B. complaisant
19. B. counsel
20. A. beside

Drill 1

1. A. affected
2. B. effect
3. A. affected
4. A. affect
5. B. effect
6. B. effect

Drill 2

1. B. a delusion
2. C. an illusion
3. A. allusions

Drill 3

1. B. complimentary
2. A. complements
3. B. complimentary
4. B. compliments
5. A. complementary

Drill 4

1. B. less
2. B. number
3. B. less
4. A. fewer
5. A. amount
6. A. fewer

Drill 5

1. B. lie
2. A. laid
3. B. lay
4. B. lain
5. A. laid
6. A. laid

215

Drill 6

1. B. past
2. A. passed
3. B. past
4. A. passed

Drill 7

1. A. rose
2. B. raised
3. A. rose
4. B. raise

Drill 8

1. B. their
2. A. there
3. C. they're

Drill 9

1. B. swum
2. B. swum
3. A. swam

Drill 10

1. properly
2. sweet
3. silently
4. slowly
5. correctly
6. Correct
7. Correct
8. quickly
9. well
10. Correct

Diction Exercises

1. A. affects
2. A. raise
3. A. principal
4. A. explicit
5. B. imminent
6. A. dessert
7. A. passed
8. A. complimentary
9. B. their
10. B. latter
11. B. conscious
12. B. averse
13. B. stationery
14. B. canvass
15. A. prescribed
16. B. hung
17. B. bear
18. B. alter

19. B. swum
20. A. laid
21. B. all ready
22. B. ingenuous
23. A. ascent
24. B. minor
25. B. baited
26. B. uninterested
27. B. every day
28. A. complement
29. B. respectively
30. B. rationale
31. B. horde
32. B. lie
33. A. allot
34. B. capitol
35. A. its
36. C. illusions
37. B. Who's
38. B. immoral
39. A. implied
40. B. flout
41. B. premiere
42. B. breath
43. B. personnel
44. A. morale
45. A. discovering
46. A. empathy
47. A. fewer
48. B. counselor
49. A. Every one
50. B. number

Wordiness

Diagnostic Test

Rewrite each group of sentences into a short sentence with the same meaning as the original group of sentences.

1. On a whim, I randomly decided to go and drive to a nearby beach that was only five minutes away from my house. I did go to that beach and it actually took me six minutes because I decided to take my dog, because I thought that it was the right thing to do.

2. Out of nowhere, an unexpected thing happened. I lost my wallet, but I think I will probably be able to find it somewhere. I will tell you that the reason is because ten minutes ago I had my wallet in my pocket and I never left the couch that I am sitting on now and is the only couch in the family room.

3. The bird, which I know to be a type of crow, is staring at me and it won't stop even when I look away for a few seconds and then look back to check if it is still staring at me. I am thinking of possibly giving the bird a small little piece of my sandwich in order to befriend the bird so that it likes me instead of not liking me.

4. My favorite person out of everyone in the world is my best friend, Samuel. He is so funny that he gets to make a living telling people funny and hilarious jokes to make people laugh. I wish with all of my heart and all of my body to do what he does for a living, but I am still happy for him and all of his success.

5. I went to the mall that has a bunch of stores that sell different things like clothes and electronics. I went with all of my family members including my brother and my dad. The reason that we went to the store is that we wanted to buy some new clothes for my little sister so she could wear them to school.

Cross out repetitive words and phrases.

6. Every single day, I try to be honest and never tell a lie.

7. I am utterly and completely sorry for not believing some of your true facts.

8. I am going to use the restroom since it currently is unoccupied and vacant.

9. I noticed here and there that there are party flyers scattered in various spots on the campus.

10. Up to this moment, I had hitherto no reason at all to be brave or courageous.

Wordiness

Polonius: "My liege and madam, to expostulate
What majesty should be, what duty is,
Why day is day, night night, and time is time,
Were nothing but to waste night, day, and time.
Therefore, since brevity is the soul of wit
And tediousness the limbs and outward flourishes,
I will be brief: your noble son is mad.
Mad call I it, for, to define true madness,
What is 't but to be nothing else but mad?
But let that go."

Gertrude: "More matter, with less art."

-SHAKESPEARE'S HAMLET

I. Be concise

When writing, it is important to be clear and concise. Include details that improve the writing and remove details that don't. Don't use a lot of words when fewer words will suffice.

Note the examples of wordy sentences followed by their revisions.

Examples: On a whim, I randomly decided to go and drive to a nearby beach that was only five minutes away from my house. I did go to that beach and it actually took me six minutes because I decided to take my dog, because I thought that it was the right thing to do.

Rewritten: On a whim, I drove with my dog to a nearby beach.

I randomly and temporarily lost my ability to see when a bird flew in front of my face and prevented me from seeing around it because it was so close to my face.

Rewritten: A flying bird temporarily blocked my view.

Drill 1 *Rewrite each sentence to make it more concise without losing its meaning.*
1. There was an alligator that I saw and it was green and it had sharp teeth and it bit multiple times into a bird that was in its vicinity.
2. I ran into someone who I hadn't seen for a long time and who used to be my friend and he told all about everything that was happening to him since we last met.
3. The place where I like more than any other to get my hair and beard cut is not going to be open anymore after its last day open on April 1st.

4. The only and best way that I can think of for you to get all of the questions correct and no questions wrong on the SAT is to study beforehand for the test.
5. I honestly wanted to make a purple kite that possibly could fly in the air and then fly the same purple kite that I made in the air.
6. Every single day, the place where I go to school keeps track of whether or not I attend the classes that I signed up for in advance.

II. Equivalent modifiers

Examples: Tautology: the bald man who lost his hair
Fixed: the man who lost his hair
Fixed: the bald man

Tautology: The test was difficult and challenging.
Fixed: The test was difficult.
Fixed: The test was challenging.

Tautology: Once in a while, I occasionally like to go to the zoo.
Fixed: Once in a while, I like to go to the zoo.
Fixed: I occasionally like to go to the zoo.

Avoid writing tautologies, which are statements that have redundant wording. Do not include multiple modifiers that mean the same thing.

Drill 2 *Cross out repetitive words and phrases.*
1. My chagrined parents were disappointed in my up to this moment poor grades in school hitherto.
2. The lion far away in the distance was dangerous and put us in peril.
3. The old man sat in silence and said not a word, even as he received news that his wife had passed away and died.
4. The skillful dancer had great prowess as she achieved noticeably far more than her peers.
5. I was amused and entertained by the hero's bravery and valor.
6. I abhorred and loathed the cafeteria's pizza, which looked like vomit or puke.

III. More redundancies

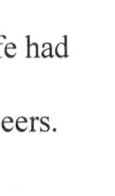

Examples: Tautology: A cold-blooded snake is now slithering past my feet.
Fixed: A ~~cold-blooded~~ snake is ~~now~~ slithering past my feet.

Tautology: I learn something new every single day.
Fixed: I learn something ~~new~~ every ~~single~~ day.

Tautology: In my mind, I decided to write an autobiography about my life.
Fixed: ~~In my mind,~~ I decided to write an autobiography ~~about my life~~.

Words shouldn't be modified by modifiers that are implied in the definition of the words.

Drill 3 *Cross out repetitive words and phrases.*
1. As an added bonus, if you call now you will receive a free gift.
2. I need advance warning of dangerous hazards in order to achieve a positive final outcome.
3. Since I know a lot about science, I am positively hopeful that I will come up with a new invention.
4. The honest truth is that I slipped and fell on some frozen ice.
5. I heard with my own ears that your husband is having an affair with a dark-haired brunette.
6. At 9:00 a.m. in the morning, I had a tuna fish sandwich.

IV. Common Tautologies

There are many possible tautologies. These are some of the more common examples that should be avoided:

- 5:00 a.m. in the morning
- added bonus
- adequate enough
- advanced warning
- again once more
- autobiography of his own life
- ATM machine
- bouquet of flowers
- cameo appearance
- close proximity
- completely eliminate
- complete opposite
- complete stop
- dark-haired brunette
- dilapidated ruins
- down under
- duplicate copy
- dry desert
- evening sunset
- exactly the same
- extreme end
- final outcome
- forward planning
- free gift
- frozen ice
- handwritten manuscript
- he made the hand-made
- heard with my own ears
- hoagie sandwich
- honest truth
- hot water heater
- in my opinion, I think
- IRA account
- jet plane
- joint cooperation
- lonely isolation
- necessary requirement
- new invention
- null and void
- over-exaggerates
- PIN number
- predictions about the future
- reply back
- return again
- sad misfortune
- serious or grave danger
- short summary
- summit at the top
- unexpected surprises
- take turns, one after the other
- tiny speck
- tuna fish

Wordiness Exercises

Rewrite each group of sentences into a short sentence with the same meaning as the original group of sentences.

1. She is right now writing from scratch an autobiography about her own life. She had spent the last seven years, two months, thirteen minutes, and twelve seconds thinking about whether or not to write the autobiography about her life, but she never actually put pen on paper and wrote one.

2. I am buying the food that has a white outer shell that you crack to get to the yellow inside part. Hens lay them and then people eat them. I am buying them at a nearby store that sells different types of foods like meats, juices, bread, pudding, milk, chips, guacamole, and eggs.

3. At 6:43 a.m. in the morning, I first opened my eyes to the outside light that shines brightly. I was so tired that I didn't want to get up so I was still laying still in my bed at 6:45 a.m. in the morning. Nevertheless, at 6:47 a.m. I put my feet on the ground and I pushed off the bed until I was standing up.

4. This game that I play on my PlayStation is not very easy and is in fact very difficult. You have to move up and down sometimes and other times you have to move left and right. The goal of the game is to avoid monsters so that you don't get eaten alive. The monsters can shoot balls of fire at you.

5. The dog, which happened to have a father that was a different breed from its mother, was walked by a boy who was still in the school that comes before high school. I went to this school when I was younger. The strange part of what happened was the dog didn't have a leash. It just followed the boy around wherever he went.

Cross out repetitive words and phrases.

6. In my opinion, I think that I need to be in close proximity of the teacher in order to hear the lesson.

7. Forward planning will help you do well and get a perfect score on your examination.

8. I went to the very end of the line and waited three hours for a ride that was boring and lackluster.

9. I remember bits and pieces of my time alone in solitary confinement.

10. The evening sunset was so beautiful and gorgeous that I completely stopped doing my homework in order to watch it with my own eyes.

Answers

(Answers may vary)

Diagnostic

1. On a whim, I drove with my dog to a nearby beach.
2. My lost wallet probably is near the family room couch.
3. To befriend a crow that is unceasingly staring at me, I might give it a sandwich crumb.
4. I yearn to become a comedian, but I am happy that my best friend Samuel is a comedian.
5. My family and I went to the shopping mall to buy school clothes for my little sister.
6. Every ~~single~~ day, I try to be honest ~~and never tell a lie~~.
7. I am utterly ~~and completely~~ sorry for not believing some of your ~~true~~ facts.
8. I am going to use the restroom since it ~~currently~~ is unoccupied ~~and vacant~~.
9. I noticed ~~here and there~~ that there are party flyers scattered ~~in various spots~~ on the campus.
10. Up to this moment, I had ~~hitherto~~ no reason ~~at all~~ to be brave ~~or courageous~~.

Drill 1

1. I saw an alligator biting a bird.
2. I caught up with an old friend.
3. My favorite barbershop is closing on April 1st.
4. You must study to get a perfect score on the SAT.
5. I wanted to make and fly a purple kite.
6. My school keeps attendance.

Drill 2

1. My ~~chagrined~~ parents were disappointed in my up to this moment poor grades in school ~~hitherto~~.
2. The lion ~~far away~~ in the distance was dangerous ~~and put us in peril~~.
3. The old man ~~sat in silence and~~ said not a word, even as he received news that his wife had ~~passed away and~~ died.
4. The skillful dancer ~~had great prowess as she~~ achieved ~~noticeably~~ far more than her peers.
5. I was amused ~~and entertained~~ by the hero's bravery ~~and valor~~.
6. I abhorred ~~and loathed~~ the cafeteria's pizza, which looked like vomit ~~or puke~~.

Drill 3

1. As a~~n added~~ bonus, if you call now you will receive a ~~free~~ gift.
2. I need ~~advance~~ warning of ~~dangerous~~ hazards in order to achieve a positive ~~final~~ outcome.
3. Since I know a lot about science, I am ~~positively~~ hopeful that I will come up with a ~~new~~ invention.
4. The ~~honest~~ truth is that I slipped and fell on some ~~frozen~~ ice.
5. I heard ~~with my own ears~~ that your husband is having an affair with a ~~dark-haired~~ brunette.
6. At 9:00 a.m. ~~in the morning~~, I had a tuna ~~fish~~ sandwich.

Exercises

1. After seven years of deliberating, she started an autobiography.
2. I am buying eggs from a nearby grocery store.
3. I tiredly woke up at 6:43 a.m., but got out of bed at 6:47 a.m.
4. In my difficult PlayStation game, I have to run away in all directions from fire-shooting monsters.
5. The middle school boy walked the mixed-breed dog without a leash.
6. ~~In my opinion~~, I think that I need to be in ~~close~~ proximity of the teacher in order to hear the lesson.
7. ~~Forward~~ planning will help you ~~do well and~~ get a perfect score on your examination.
8. I went to the ~~very~~ end of the line and waited three hours for a ride that was ~~boring and~~ lackluster.
9. I remember bits ~~and pieces~~ of my time ~~alone~~ in solitary confinement.
10. The ~~evening~~ sunset was so beautiful ~~and gorgeous~~ that I ~~completely~~ stopped doing my homework in order to watch it ~~with my own eyes~~.

Third Cumulative Review

For each sentence, determine whether it is grammatically correct. If it is grammatically incorrect, identify the type of error:

Verb - V   Subject Verb Agreement - A   Pronoun - P

Fragment - F   Misplaced Modifier - M   Lack of Parallel Structure - L

Punctuation - C   Run-On Sentence - R   Diction - D   Wordiness - W

(V, A, P, F, M, L, C, R, D, W)

*Improper comparisons are part of Lack of Parallel Structure

*The punctuation of the restrictive and nonrestrictive element is part of Punctuation

1. The school committee accepted the school principal's draconian decision to cut the school budget in half; however, he later relented his recommendation and asked the committee to revert to the original budget.

2. The deadline for signing up for the SAT is one month prior to the date. In the event of a missed deadline, a student might be able to take the test at a test center other than that of his local high school; a center that is seventy miles away that happens to have a seat available.

3. Shakespeare's play *Macbeth* is the tragic and lurid tale of a great warrior who invites the King of Scotland to his castle home, where at night, together with his wife, Lady Macbeth, murders in cold blood the sleeping Duncan, who has no inkling that he is the guest of a host bent on murder.

4. Years ago the Patriots had a coach who was well known for his rigidity in insisting that players continue to perform in the game irregardless of their injuries.

5. The boy in the back of the class always vexed and bothered the Spanish teacher, who one day sought revenge by hurling his way first pieces of chalk and then an eraser, all of which hit the intended target.
6. Now that the novice in French had finished a short summary of the grammar of the language he thinks he is ready to fly to Paris and test his savvy.
7. Dubai, otherwise known as the city of gold, has numerous activities for tourists to take part in, such as skydiving, traveling across the desert, and they can walk around the enormous mall.
8. After witnessing from the window of a nearby skyscraper the September 11 attacks on the World Trade Center, the foreign journalist, overwhelmed by what she had beheld, found it difficult to sit down and type up her report of the incident.
9. The toothache that the patient was suffering became so acute that the pain effected his work; he had to leave his office, stop work, and rest until the dentist could find time to attend to the emergency.
10. Before the hapless student went to the school to take her first SAT, she hadn't scarcely opened a book that gave advice about the test and gave examples that showed what the test would be like.
11. In the film *The Illusionist*, the clever magician after successfully evading the authorities retreats to an obscure part of the countryside in pursuit of a sanctuary for himself and his wife.
12. My old, blue sweater that for many years I kept in the closet adjacent to my brothers' hats, is now a moth-eaten and haunting reminder that I should have stored it in a sealed box with mothballs.

13. "Its a Long Way to Tipperary" was a battle song popular during World War I, but despite the passage of a century, can still be heard today by veterans of all wars when the bands play patriotic songs in their honor.

14. To flout his intelligence, my friend, Jack, took a test that was designed for students twice his age.

15. My math teacher's teaching style is far more entertaining than any other teacher's.

16. The vice principal of the school told the teachers that he did not approve of how, after the fire drill, the students ascended up the stairway to the second floor with such speed that they almost trampled one another.

17. Permitting monopolies and cartels to grow unchecked relegate every competing company to a position in which it sees a diminishing market share.

18. In regards to the new SAT, which was introduced to students two years ago, most students have found that they now have to learn the basics of English grammar which appear in the section called Writing Skills.

19. President Donald Trump, along with his wife, Melania, is planning a trip to France to talk about pivotal, crucial topics: global warming, NATO, and trade agreements.

20. While driving to school, I realized that I had forgotten to bring my lunch, however, I didn't have time to go back and get it.

21. Jeff and his family, throughout the four seasons of the year, visits the memorial very often.

22. The Prime Minister of Great Britain, Theresa May, begun the negotiations to leave the European Union three years ago, but Britain's exit from the Union has been delayed because of an impasse in Parliament.

23. In accosting and vehemently reproaching Gertrude, Hamlet elicited immediate fear in her eavesdropping advisor, Polonius, who, hiding behind an arras, became agitated and vocal in wanting to help the shamed Gertrude.

24. Do you see the boy, sitting on the table, that is wobbly?

25. An I.T. employee who was relocating to another branch of his company taught her replacement how to log in to the company system, how to deliver critical monthly reports to superiors, and how to manage industry-specific threats to firewalls.

26. Fighting until his last breathe, my father died very heroically.

27. When the President of the United States had ordered a strike on an Iranian facility, he needed to send a message to his general in charge of the operation that gave the general authority to initiate the action.

28. Through dedicating himself to hockey practice and because he showed immense interest in the sport, Bobby won the attention of many Division I coaches.

29. She wants to run for President. That means that she will need to garner the support of many people.

30. The candidate with the highest poll numbers in the Democratic Party had not hardly announced his candidacy when he was attacked by the less moderate elements in his party who were reacting to how even a week after his announcement he still led all the other candidates in the public's opinion.

31. While campaigning in the upcoming Presidential Primaries for 2020, the front runner for the Democratic Party has taken political positions that are different than those of his rivals; his are conservative, but he may soon feel pressured to take stands that are more progressive so as not to appear out of step and old-fashioned.

32. Warfare by attrition once the staple of many militaries has been replaced by superior technological methods.

33. In a diary written by one of the pioneers who went west to settle the new and unknown territory opened up by the Louisiana Purchase, a mother of three writes that the way of traveling long days under a hot sun in wagons, along with the habit of sleeping at night under cold skies unprotected from the elements and wild animals, was an experience as exhausting as it was exhilarating.

34. Obscured behind a shriveled bush in the desert lay a suitcase. A twenty-two inch by fourteen-inch by nine-inch metallically layered piece of luggage containing some of the spoils of the traficantes who had plagued this dry region peddling deadly narcotics accompanied by rampant extortions.

35. Although his reputation for veracity, reliability, and perseverance was not as great as his rival, nevertheless Boris Johnson was favored to become the next Prime Minister of Great Britain, perhaps because of such other qualities he possessed in abundance as dynamism, mercurial wit, boundless good nature, and strong rapport with everyday working people.

36. All of my friends except for Michael and I are going to the city.

37. After a long day at work, I heard on my car radio that the president might pardon Josh Fredrick.

38. Life's but a walking shadow, a poor player. That struts and frets his hour upon the stage, and then is heard no more.

39. The ocean temperature in the water off the coast of the balmy Canary Islands is expected to become cooler during the winter months, but infinitesimally less so than that off the frigid coast of Maine.

40. At the lake house party, a group of academically successful and studious students were apprehended by the police for underage drinking. The students' futures would be marred and damaged indefinitely.

41. No matter how hard I try, my grades never seem to raise high enough to satisfy my parents.

42. Having worked hard and succeeded in difficult classes, Ella's academic transcript shows that she is extremely well qualified.

43. The researchers are hoping to effect a cure for the contagious disease, which easily spreads from person to person.

44. In *Hamlet*, soon after Queen Gertrude had drank the poisoned cup, she began to choke, and in her death spasm motioned to her son the drink; Prince Hamlet grabbed a poisoned sword and in revenge stabbed Claudius, the King and culpable poisoner.

45. Every day I learn something new, today, I learned how to solve a Rubik's Cube.

46. Sweden, as well as Denmark, Norway, Iceland, and Finland, are part of Scandinavia.

47. Upon hearing a loud screeching sound, I ran to my favorite hiding spot: under the stairs.

48. Despite running as fast as he could, Usain Bolt who ran 100 meters in 9.58 seconds, couldn't catch up to the moving train.

49. The local restaurant often sees a significant increase in business during football season. Especially when the Patriots are in the playoffs. Football is the sport with the greatest impact on commerce.

50. The milk is spoiled, you should throw it out.

51. She placed the beautiful golden crown on her head, which was much too large.

52. *To Kill a Mockingbird* Harper Lee's most popular novel is still used in schools today more than fifty years after it was written.

53. George Kennan developed a strategy to halt communism that was called containment.

54. "I can't find your car keys," I sobbed, "I thought I left them on the counter, but I already looked there."

55. After her years in the White House, Hillary Clinton, formally the First Lady of the United States, moved with her husband to a home in Chappaqua, New York, which served as a base from which to launch her campaign to be a United States senator.

56. The excavations at Pompeii, unlike Rome, to uncover the remains of the debris covered city buried from the eruption of Mount Vesuvius two thousand years ago, yielded the discovery of a statue of Apollo, which now restored to its original glory stands proudly for all to see just below the columns of the eponymous temple of Apollo, behind which looms Vesuvius.

57. During his recent speech, the politician expressed his belief that monopolistic pharmaceutical companies must be obligated to lower prices, to list drug prices on television commercials, and elicit investment in the fight against the opioid crisis.

58. To get to the only place where I feel safe, I ran through the forest and climbed over a fence.

59. My best friend, Sandy, got a very high score on the SAT, in fact, she scored higher than everyone else in our school.

60. Each modification, whether serving to alter the color, texture, or engraving of the device, cost an additional fifty dollars.

61. Abraham Lincoln, the president of the United States during the Civil War, understood the severity of internal threats: "America will never be destroyed from the outside. If we falter and lose our freedoms, it will be because we destroyed ourselves."

62. In preparing the many hundreds of sentences for this book, sentences that would challenge students to pay strict attention to parts of speech, parts of a sentence, and phrases and clauses, the amount of hours involved took its toll on the test maker's patience.

63. The man, who runs our company, is currently on vacation in the Bahamas, but he will be back in the office on Wednesday.

64. John Mayer, walking onto the stage, evoked a loud lengthy applause.

65. My friend complimented me; however, I couldn't hear her.

66. After climbing endless timeworn stone stairs to reach the medieval hilltop city of Toledo, the tourists said they were tired, but when they finally returned to their hotel in Madrid, they felt so exhilarated by the grandeur and panorama they saw, they said they were not tired at all.

67. Learning to speak Spanish in a classroom during a school year will not remove a student from the artificiality of such a setting, nor provide a student the kind of priceless linguistic experience he would have gained if he would have lived for a month with a host family in Spain.

68. Although Michael may be better than me at mathematics, I still scored higher on the trigonometry exam than him.

69. After finishing my dessert I drove up to visit my mother, who looked ten years older than she did yesterday.

70. The mountain climbers carried there backpacks beyond the timber line to the summit where in spite of the high winds, low temperatures, and exposure to the elements there, pitched tent. Shelter was only provided them by the thin canvas of the tents.

71. My mother frequently talked about her love of the great outdoors; hence, I decided to take her to my favorite camping site where we would be five miles away from the nearest town.

72. According to conservative pundits, socialism, as an economic system, has failed repeatedly to produce positive results; these critics say that as a seductive moral doctrine, socialism has succeeded in exploiting vulnerable human beings.

73. The committee convened to address the election violations in the conference room.

74. Centuries ago a soldier, turning traitor during a battle but apprehended before he had a chance to flee to the enemy side, would be hung for his treachery.

75. When I went shopping at the supermarket, hoping to find in the cheese section Brie or Camembert, I found there instead less authentic French brands available than in the past, though available there were more cheeses that looked French but were just American imitations.

76. The pressure was mounting and his graduation depended on his calculus final, so for an entire week Michael studied he was ready for his test.

77. Morrissey was the lead singer of the Smiths they were a pioneering alternative band with numerous hit songs on both the U.S. and U.K. charts.

78. Following a traditional labor distribution system, the manager oversaw the project, the employee did the work.

79. After excessive rains caused floods to run over the main road of the town, the superintendent decided to accept students from attending school if they lived on or near the road affected.

80. The punch-drunk boxer became so exhausted by the eighth round of the match that he seemed like an automaton just going through the motions in a holding pattern until the gong sounded and thus in effect ended his ordeal.

Third Cumulative Review Answers

1. Correct
2. C - colon instead of semicolon
3. Correct
4. D - regardless
5. W - vexed and bothered
6. V - has finished
7. L - "and they can walk" should be in the gerund form: and walking
8. W - type up
9. D - affected
10. V - hadn't scarcely
11. P - comma after illusionist and authorities
12. C - No comma between old and blue
13. C - "It's a Long Way to Tipperary"
14. D - flaunt
15. Correct
16. W - ascended up
17. A - permitting... relegates
18. D - in regard to (in "regards" to doesn't exist)
19. W - pivotal, crucial
20. R - However is not a conjunction. Therefore, the sentence needs a period or semicolon after lunch
21. A - Jeff and his family... visit

22. *V - began*

23. *Correct*

24. *C - That is wobbly is restrictive. Therefore, there shouldn't be a comma before that.*

25. *Correct*

26. *D - Breath*

27. *V - President of the United States ordered*

28. *L - "dedicating himself to hockey practice" is not parallel to "because he showed immense interest"*

29. *P - Ambiguous reference: "That" lacks a clear antecedent*

30. *V - had not hardly*

31. *D - differs from*

32. *C - comma after attrition, militaries*

33. *Correct*

34. *F - the second cluster of words is an incomplete thought*

35. *L - as great as the reputation of his rival*

36. *P - except for Michael and me*

37. *Correct*

38. *F - the second cluster of words is an incomplete thought*

39. *Correct*

40. *W - academically successful and studious*

41. *D - rise*

42. *M - "Ella's academic transcript" did not work hard*

43. *W - Contagious means the same thing as easily spreads from person to person.*

44. V - had drunk

45. R - Every day I learn something new and today, I learned how to solve a Rubik's Cube are independent clauses joined by a comma

46. A - Sweden... is

47. Correct

48. C - Who ran 100 meters in 9.58 seconds is a nonrestrictive element. Therefore, there should be a comma after Usain Bolt.

49. F - the second cluster of words is an incomplete thought

50. R - There are two independent clauses connected by a comma

51. M - the crown was "too large," not "her head"

52. C - Harper Lee's most popular novel is a nonrestrictive phrase. Therefore, there should be commas before and after it.

53. M - "Communism" was not called "containment"

54. R - when a quotation is split into two complete sentences, there should be a period after whatever introduces the quotations

55. D - formerly

56. L - unlike those at Rome

57. E - "and elicit" must be in the infinitive form

58. Correct

59. R - In fact is not a conjunction. Therefore, the sentence needs a period or semicolon after SAT.

60. A - modification... costs

61. Correct

62. D - "the amount of hours" should be "the number of hours"

63. C - Who runs our company is restrictive. Therefore, the commas that are before and after it should be removed.

64. C - There should be a comma between loud and lengthy, because the order of those adjectives doesn't matter

65. Correct

66. V - grandeur and panorama they had seen

67. V - if he had lived

68. P - than he

69. C - There should be a comma after the phrase after eating dessert, because it is a modifying phrase that begins the sentence.

70. D - their

71. C - Assuming that I have only one favorite camping site, the clause where we would be five miles away from the nearest town is nonrestrictive. Therefore, there should be a comma after site.

72. Correct

73. M - the "election violations" did not occur in the conference room

74. D - hanged

75. D - fewer

76. R - The pressure was mounting and his graduation depended on his calculus final, so for an entire week Michael studied. He was ready for the test .... OR The pressure was mounting and his graduation depended on his calculus final, so for an entire week Michael studied; he was ready for the test.

77. *R - Morrissey was the lead singer of the Smiths. They were a pioneering alternative band with numerous hit songs on both the U.S. and U.K. charts...OR Morrisey was the lead singer of the Smiths, who were a pioneering alternative band with numerous hit songs on both the U.S. and U.K. charts.*

78. *R - Following a traditional labor distribution system, the manager oversaw the project. The employee did the work. .... OR Following a traditional labor distribution system, the manager oversaw the project while the employee did the work.*

79. *D - excepted, not accepted*

80. *Correct*

TRANSITIONS IN WRITING PARAGRAPHS

Words or phrases that add to an idea, explain the causation behind it, or in contrast pivot away from it.

Transitions

Diagnostic Test

Pick the letter of the best option.

1. I lost my son in the middle of the city. (A. In fact, B. Unfortunately, C. Nevertheless, D. Thus,) he found his way home.

2. Apple recently came under fire for its admission that it slows older phones. (A. In any case, B. Additionally, C. Still, D. Accordingly,) Apple has very strong customer satisfaction.

3. Amazon Go's first cashier-free convenience store was very profitable. (A. Indeed, B. In fact, C. Therefore, D. In particular,) Amazon Go decided to launch another cashier-free convenience store on August 27th.

4. Google's pursuit of innovation has led to many subsidiaries. (A. For example, B. Hence, C. Moreover, D. Specifically,) Google created Waymo, a self-driving technology development company.

5. Most physical trainers admit that nutrition is at least as important to your health as exercise. (A. Luckily, B. Thus, C. However, D. Because this is true,) it came as no surprise when my gym opened a nutritional snack bar.

6. NASA is most famous for landing the first man on the moon. (A. Furthermore, B. However, C. Above all, D. Hence,) it also studies the environment.

7. Our students can have a tutoring lesson in their homes. (A. Furthermore, B. Meanwhile, C. Nonetheless, D. In other words,) they can learn without leaving their front door.

8. I am not used to being responsible for so many students. (A. In fact, B. First of all, C. Conversely, D. To summarize,) the largest class size that I've ever taught is sixteen students.

9. My parents double checked to make sure that I had finished my homework. (A. However, B. Similarly, C. Thus, D. After all,) they want me to succeed.

10. I prayed to God to save my dying aunt. (A. Finally, B. Chiefly, C. Unfortunately, D. Accordingly,) she passed away last night.

Transitions

Transitions must correctly describe the relationship between sentences or ideas. There are three main relationship categories: addition, causation, and contrast.

I. Addition

If the second sentence or idea adds on to the first one, then the relationship is additive.

A. Extra Information

The following transition words are used for adding information:

also is used to add information

additionally is used to add new information

furthermore is used to add to or support the previous statement

in addition is used to add information connected to the previous statement

in fact is used to add more detailed information

indeed is used to add information that strengthens the previous information

likewise is used to add similar information

moreover is used to add to or support the previous statement

namely is used to add specific information

similarly is used to add similar information

specifically is used to add specific information

Examples: My best friend told me that the pool was too cold. *In fact*, the temperature was only 40° F.

Jake was late to his dentist appointment. *Similarly*, I was late to my orthodontist appointment.

B. Examples

Use **for example** and **for instance** to introduce examples of the previous statements.

Example: My brother always finds a way to disappoint me. *For example*, he recently showed up to my birthday party drunk.

C. Emphasis

The following transitions add emphasis:

above all is used to introduce the most important point

chiefly is used to introduce the main or most important point

in particular is used to add information that applies especially to one person or thing

markedly is used to introduce clearly noticeable information

noticeably is used to introduce clearly noticeable information

particularly is used to add information that applies especially to one person or thing

Examples: *Above all*, we value dedication.

Noticeably, the man lost all hope after his wife passed away.

The boy irritates me. *In particular*, I can't stand his whiny voice.

D. Restatement

The following transitions introduce a restatement of what came before:

after all is used to introduce a statement that supports or helps explain the previous statement

all things considered is used to introduce a judgment that takes all facts into account

by and large is used to introduce a statement that is mostly but not completely true

in any case/event is used to introduce a more important statement that supports or corrects the previous statement

in brief is used to introduce a short summary

in conclusion is used to introduce a conclusion

in essence is used to introduce the most important or central aspect of something

in other words is used to introduce another way of saying something

in short is used to introduce a short summary

in summary is used to introduce a summary

to sum up is used to introduce a summary

to summarize is used to introduce a summary

Examples: My teacher recently quit her job and moved to Australia. *In other words*, I will never see or hear my teacher again.

Six months ago, I was diagnosed with a torn ACL. To get better, I have been going to the gym to build up strength in my knee. Unfortunately, my progress has stalled. *In summary*, I am losing my six-month-long fight to recover from a torn ACL.

E. Sequence

The following transitions are used to introduce something that is part of a sequence:

afterwards is used to introduce something that happens after something else

at first is used to introduce the first element in a series

at the same time is used to introduce a statement that happens at the same time as the previous

finally is used to introduce the last element in a series or something that happens after a long period of time

first of all is used to introduce the first element in a series

firstly is used to introduce the first element in a series

for now is used to introduce something that is true right now

in time is used to introduce something that eventually will be true

later on is used to introduce something that comes after the previous statement or in the future

meanwhile is used to introduce something that happens at the same time as the previous; the second statement can add to or contrast with the previous

next is used to introduce something that comes immediately after the previous statement

simultaneously is used to introduce something that happens at the same time as the previous

subsequently is used to introduce something that follows in time or order

to begin with is used to introduce the first stage of something

then is used to introduce something that comes logically after the previous statement

Examples: *To begin with*, preheat the oven to 420° F. *Then*, take the chicken nuggets out of the fridge.

My brother is on vacation in the Bahamas. *Meanwhile*, I am stuck in traffic on the highway.

F. Generalizations

The following transitions are used for generalizations.

as a rule is used to introduce something that usually happens or is a rule

for the most part is used to introduce describe something that is mostly true

frequently is used to introduce something that frequently happens

generally is used to introduce something that happens on most occasions

normally is used to introduce the usual or conventional way

ordinarily is used to introduce something that is normally true

sometimes is used to introduce something that could happen

usually is used to introduce something that is more likely than not to happen

Examples: *Ordinarily*, I don't give money to strangers.

Sometimes, I get so exhausted that I pass out.

II. Causation

The following transitions are used for when one statement or idea causes another statement or idea:

accordingly is used to introduce a fact or situation that is a result of the previous statement

as a result is used to introduce a result of the previous action or event

consequently is used to introduce something that is a consequence of the previous statement

for this purpose is used to introduce the reason derived from the previous statement

for this reason is used to introduce something that is true because of the previous statement

hence is used to introduce formally a result of the previous action or event

therefore is used to introduce something that is true because of the previous statement

thus is used to introduce something that is true because of the previous statement

Examples: When I drove to the restaurant, I did not see an available parking spot. *For this reason*, I decided to drive to another restaurant.

I am not feeling well. *Hence*, I will not be at work today.

III. Contrast

The following transitions are used for when statements or ideas conflict with each other:

conversely is used to introduce something that reverses the previous statement

despite this is used to introduce something that is true even though the previous statement is true

however is used to introduce something that contrasts with the previous statement

in contrast is used to introduce something that contrasts with the previous statement

nevertheless is used to introduce something that is true even though the previous statement is true

nonetheless is used to introduce something that is true even though the previous statement is true

on the other hand is used to introduce an alternative point of view

still is used to introduce something that is true even though the previous statement is true

yet is used to introduce something that is true even though the previous statement is true

Examples: If the principal wants to talk to you, it could mean that you are in trouble. *Conversely*, it could mean that he wants to commend you for doing well in school.

My girlfriend broke up with me last night. *Nevertheless*, I love her more than I ever have.

My mother forgot to pick me up from band practice. *On the other hand*, I had an opportunity to make new friends.

IV. Identify the relationship

To determine the best transition, first determine the relationship between sentences. First, narrow the relationship down between addition, causation, and contrast. Recall that transitions that involve addition are used when ideas add on to each other, transitions that involve causation are used when one statement or idea causes another statement or idea, and transitions that involve contrast are used when statements or ideas conflict with each other.

Examples: I decided to go try out for the school play. I couldn't find where the tryouts were being held.

The above sentences conflict with each other, and so they should be joined with a transition that indicates contrast such as *nevertheless*:
I decided to go try out for the school play. *Nevertheless*, I couldn't find where the tryouts were being held.

I recently got accepted to Harvard Law School. I plan to attend the school next semester.

The second sentence is a result of the first sentence, and so they should be joined with a transition that indicates causation such as *therefore*:
I recently got accepted to Harvard Law School. *Therefore*, I plan to attend the school next semester.

My best friend is moving to Toronto in order to start a new job as a web developer. He will be over three hundred miles away from me.

The second sentence adds on to the first sentence, and so they should be joined with a transition that indicates addition:
My best friend is moving to Toronto in order to start a new job as a web developer. *In other words*, he will be over three hundred miles away from me.

For transitions that involve addition, it is important to use the correct type. Recall that the types of transitions that involve addition are extra information, examples, emphasis, restatement, sequence, and generalizations.

In the above example in which the friend moves to Toronto, the second sentence is a restatement of the first, and so *in other words* is a good transition. Note that replacing *in other words* with *at first* or *for example* wouldn't make sense, because they are the wrong type of transitions that involve addition.

Drill 1 *Determine whether the sentences should be joined by an addition, causation, or contrast transition. For addition transitions, specify whether they should be extra information, examples,*

emphasis, restatement, sequence, or generalizations.
1. Add chocolate syrup to your milk. Stir until they are mixed thoroughly.
2. I forgot to do last night's homework assignment. The teacher gave us a surprise extension on the assignment.
3. The job has very difficult to meet requirements. Applicants must have a Ph.D. and at least ten years of experience in a relevant field.
4. The boy was caught smoking marijuana on the school campus. He was expelled.
5. I ran faster than I had ever run before. I ran so fast that my gym teacher had to pull me aside to tell me to slow down.
6. I thought that *Zoolander 2* was terrible. I was not surprised when it did not win an Oscar.

V. Other ways to begin a sentence

We also can begin a sentence with a relevant adverb or phrase.

Examples: *Unfortunately*, I will not be able to attend your wedding.

True, the test was more difficult than normal, but you still should have tried your best.

Even today, scientists have trouble conveying their findings to the public.

When picking the right way to start a sentence, consider everything you've learned. Avoid misplaced modifiers, wordiness, and transitions that incorrectly specify the relationships between sentences.

Transition Exercises

Pick the letter of the best option.

1. I thought that I didn't have a chance of being accepted into Harvard Law School. (A. Finally, B. Hence, C. Despite this, D. Subsequently,) I was accepted and will start in the fall.

2. Phillips Academy's motto, Non Sibi, means "not for oneself." (A. Therefore, B. In other words, C. On the other hand, D. In the abstract,) one should be selfless.

3. David Blaine has created innovative magic tricks that captivate audiences. (A. In essence, B. Nonetheless, C. Finally, D. Moreover,) his performing style keeps audiences in suspense.

4. There was a lot of controversy over the role of the superdelegates in the 2016 Democratic primary. (A. Nevertheless, B. To sum up, C. Hence, D. Additionally,) the primary winner, Hillary Clinton, received a higher share of the popular vote than Bernie Sanders did.

5. Our country is increasingly relying on diverse forms of energy, including solar and wind. (A. Still, B. Nevertheless, C. Meanwhile, D. Therefore,) two of the fastest growing jobs are solar photovoltaic installers and wind turbine service technicians.

6. Follow-up studies found that people who tried the keto diet were less likely to stick to the diet. (A. Evidently, B. However, C. Lastly, D. Thus,) the diet required too great a change for people to handle.

7. Fifty years ago, I paid for my college tuition by working a part-time job. (A. Therefore, B. Today, C. Nevertheless, D. Ironically,) college has become much more expensive and the price is constantly rising.

8. Technology companies like Amazon and Google are famous for their innovations. (A. Hence, B. Moreover, C. Still, D. Lastly,) some potential investors are worried by the companies' lack of a dividend.

9. The September 11 attacks, conducted by the terrorist group al-Qaeda, killed 2,996 people and wounded over 6,000 others. (A. Accordingly, B. Despite this, C. Meanwhile, D. True,) people will still remember the attacks decades after it happened.

10. Math was always my least favorite subject in school. (A. However, B. Consequently, C. To sum up, D. In particular,) I was surprised that I enjoyed Geometry so much.

Answers

Diagnostic

1. C. Nevertheless,
2. C. Still,
3. C. Therefore,
4. A. For example,
5. B. Thus, (*Because this is true* is more verbose and uses an ambiguous *this*)
6. B. However,
7. D. In other words,
8. A. In fact,
9. D. After all,
10. C. Unfortunately,

Drill 1

1. Addition, sequence
2. Contrast
3. Addition, examples
4. Causation
5. Addition, extra information
6. Causation

Exercises

1. C. Despite this,
2. B. In other words,
3. D. Moreover,
4. A. Nevertheless,
5. D. Therefore,
6. A. Evidently,
7. B. Today,
8. C. Still,
9. A. Accordingly,
10. B. Consequentl

English Abused

A student striving to be an effective writer needs practice putting his thoughts on paper. Whether in letters, journal entries, reports, compositions, or essays —he will hone his skills over time, learning by doing. To undergird his progress, however, he should know the fundamentals of English: its structure, grammar, syntax, usage, and idiosyncrasies. To avoid pitfalls that can drag him down and to make his work sharper and stronger, the aspiring writer might well avail himself of English Abused.

Crafting Sharper, Stronger English
The Series

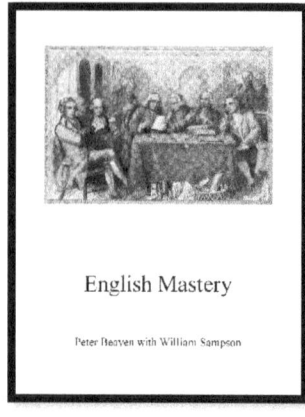

www.ingramcontent.com/pod-product-compliance
Lightning Source LLC
Chambersburg PA
CBHW080547230426
43663CB00015B/2739

9781327489272